the
BIG
small show

12/11/14 - 1/25/15

Victory Hall Drawing Rooms

180 Grand St. Jersey City

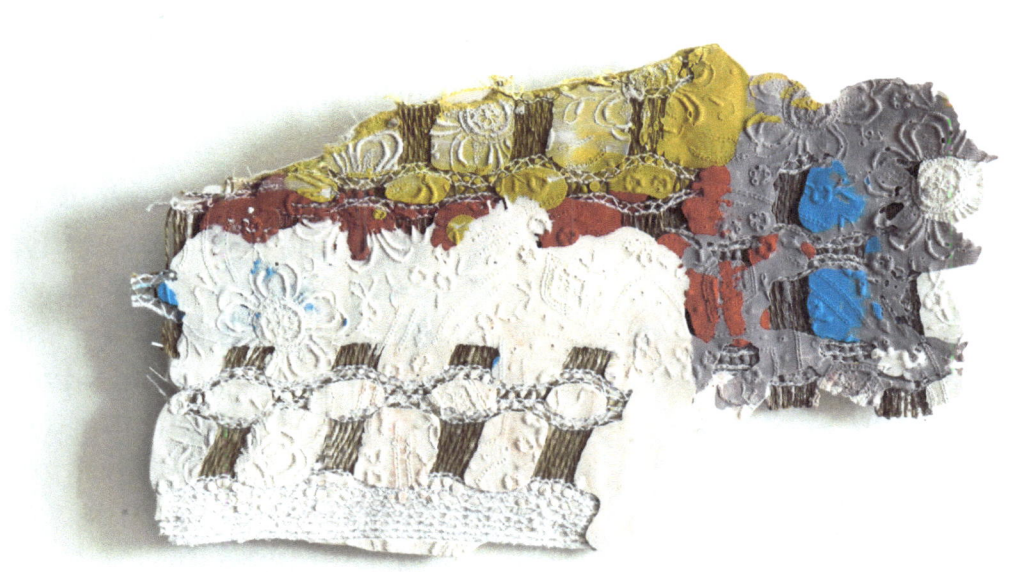

Sylvia Schwartz, *Falling Pigment Series* 2, 2013 9 x 6 inches

THE BIG SMALL PAINTING SHOW

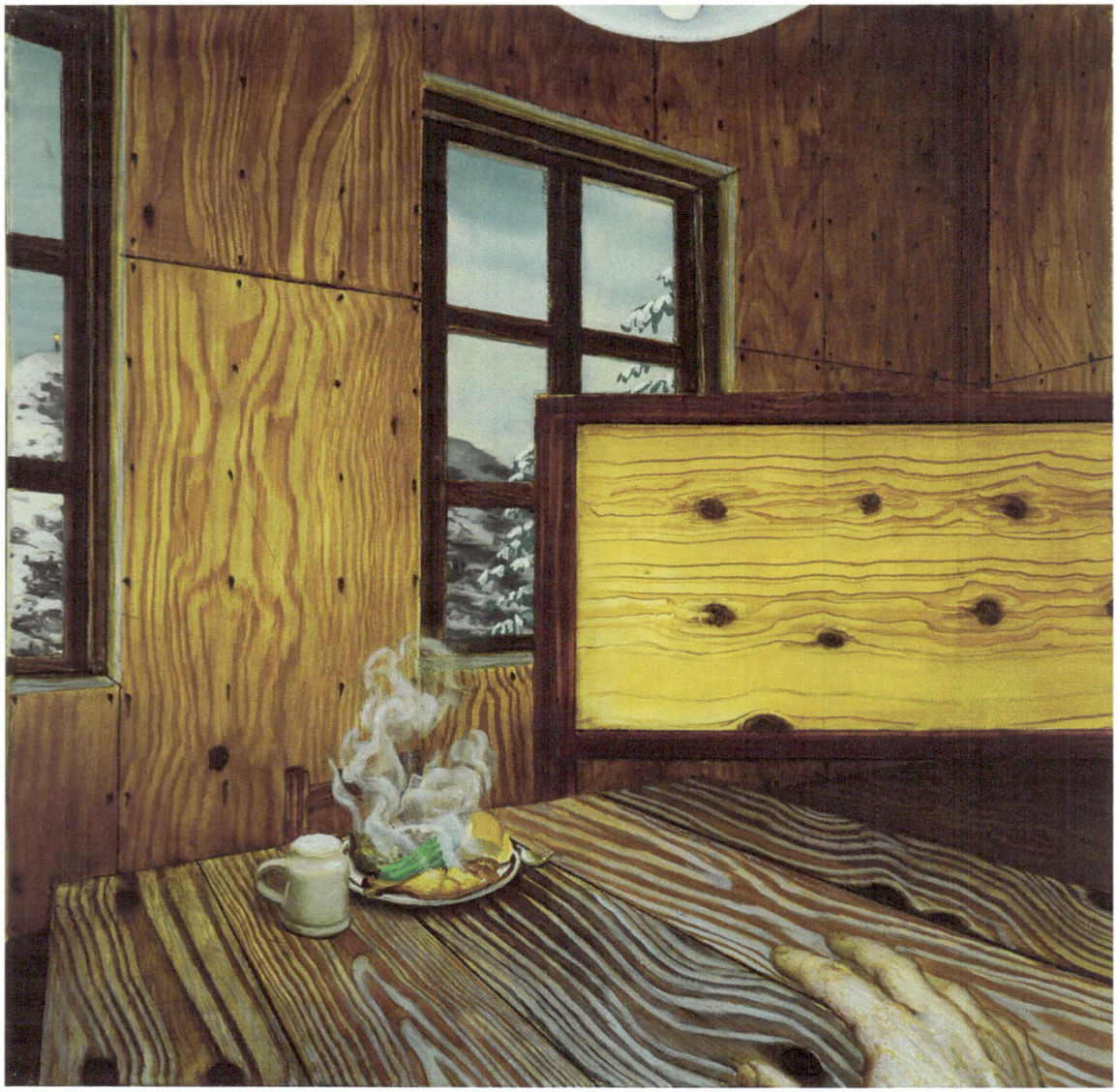

John Jacobsmeyer, *No Pudding,* oil on canvas 2013 12 x 12 inches

Alan Walker, Alberte Bernier, Barbara M. Marks, Bette Blank, Bill Stamos, Binnie Birstein, Buck Henri, Candy le Sueur, Caridad Kennedy, Cecile Brunswick, Dana Kane, Deirdre Kennedy, Eileen Ferara, Eliot Markell, Ellen Hackl Fagan, Ellie Murphy, Enrico Gomez, Eveline Luppi, Fabricio Suarez, Fermin Mendoza, Fran Shalom, Gail Winbury, Gilbert Giles, Glenn Garver, Greg Brickey, Greg Letson, Gregory Stone, Heidi Curko, Ian Mack, Ibou Ndoye, Jane Dell, Jeanne Tremel, John Jacobsmeyer, Kevin McCaffrey, Laurie Riccadonna, Len Merlo, Lisa Ficarelli-Halpern, Loura van der Meule, Manuel Macarrulla, Marianne DeAngelis, Meg Atkinson, Michael Ensminger, Michelle Doll, Patricia Satterlee, Pauline Chernichaw, Peter Bill, Richard White, Robert Otto Epstein, Robert Preston, Robin Feld, Robyn Ellenbogen, Ruth Hiller, Ryan DaWalt, Stephen Cimini, Steve Singer, Sylvia Schwartz, Terri Amig, Theresa DeSalvio, Vincent Romaniello

THE BIG SMALL WORKS SHOW

Aileen Bassis, Alice Harrison, Anne Trauben, Austin Thomas, Barbara Stork, Beth Dary, Carol Radsprecher, Cheryl Gross, Chris Vivas, Christina Tenaglia, Dasha Bazanova, Eileen Hoffman, Ellen Hackl Fagan, Gianluca Bianchino, Helena Starcevic, James Prez, Jaynie Crimmins, Jaz Graf, Jeremy Coleman Smith, Joanne Howard, Jodie Fink, Julie McHargue, Koo Seunghwui, Lady MacCrady, Maggie Ens, Margaret Weber, Megan Klim, Mollie Thonneson, Peter Emerick, PS Press Peter Duffin, PS Press Sam Larson, Ryan Sarah Murphy, Suzan Shutan, Tim Main

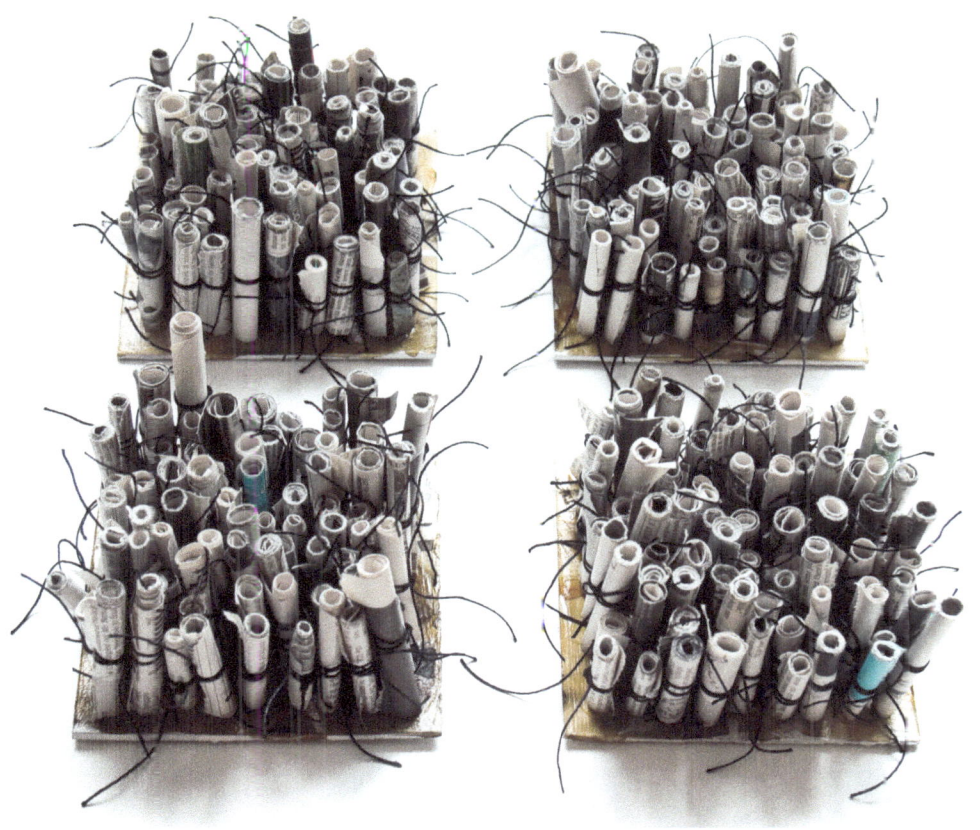

Jaz Graf, World View II, mixed media book

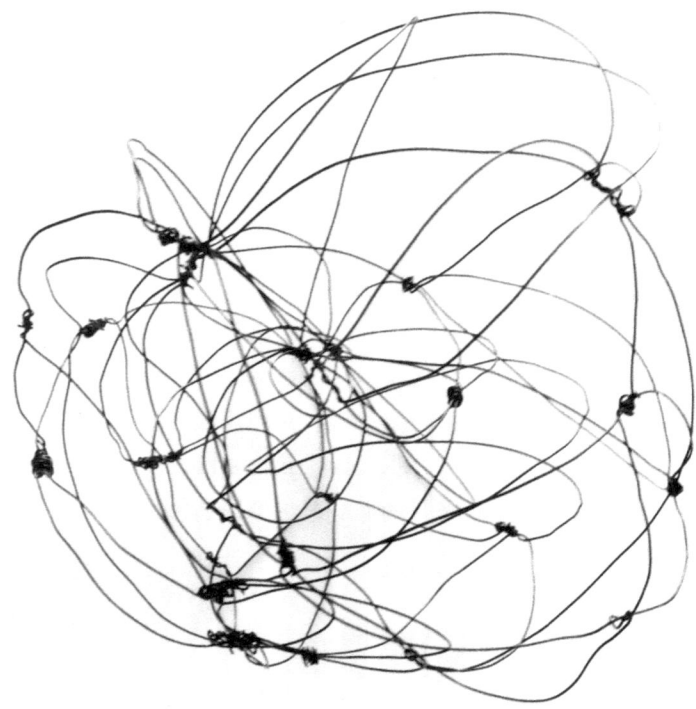

Anne Trauben , 1081, wire

 The Big Small Show 2014 represents a sampling of recent, innovative works by ninety artists in the New Jersey/New York metropolitan area, and it is clearly expressive of the exciting level of energy and interaction that is happening among the artists included here, an indicator of the activity of our larger arts community as well. For all of us who have been developing Victory Hall DRAWING ROOMS as an art center since 2012 it also is a celebration, the harvest of our continual efforts to make a place for creative visual artists in Jersey City, believing that when the Arts flourish, the city will also flourish.

This event marks a celebratory return to occasional use of the Victory Hall location for our arts non-profit organization. Victory Hall started as an arts center as the events of 9-11 were occurring in 2001, and for the next six years provided a place where dance companies, theater groups, spoken word and poetry, filmmakers and classes in arts and martial arts could connect to thousands of community members each year, as well as producing consistent, large-scale art exhibitions featuring hundreds of area artists.

When the building was transformed to a Preschool due to the growth of the school and area population, Victory Hall Inc. continued it's programming in public places and in institutions like the Jersey City Museum until founding Drawing Rooms in 2012. After a six-month rehab due to Hurricane Sandy damage, Victory Hall Drawing Rooms has been steadily presenting exhibitions in the former Our Lady of Czestochowa convent building since May 2013. The multiple cell-like rooms have become a uniquely beautiful place for painting, drawing and constructions to be experienced by the community.

Thanks to all the artists in this exhibition for their wonderful works, and to all the artists, musicians, teachers, business people, students, visitors and everyone who is part of what we do throughout the year. Special thanks to Pat Rubino and Keungsuk Sexton, present and past Board Presidents, our board members, Planning Committee and my wife, Jill Scipione for their unflagging support and guidance, to all our sponsors and financial supporters, and to Fr. Tom Ciba and the OLC parish and School.

Curator Anne Trauben has done an amazing job of tirelessly seeking out and gathering paintings, sculpture, drawings, artist-made books, and most importantly people who make art and people who support art from across both rivers and north to Connecticut.
We welcome you all to the Big Small Painting and Big Small Works Show for 2014.

James Pustorino
Director, Victory Hall DRAWING ROOMS
Executive Director, Victory Hall Inc.

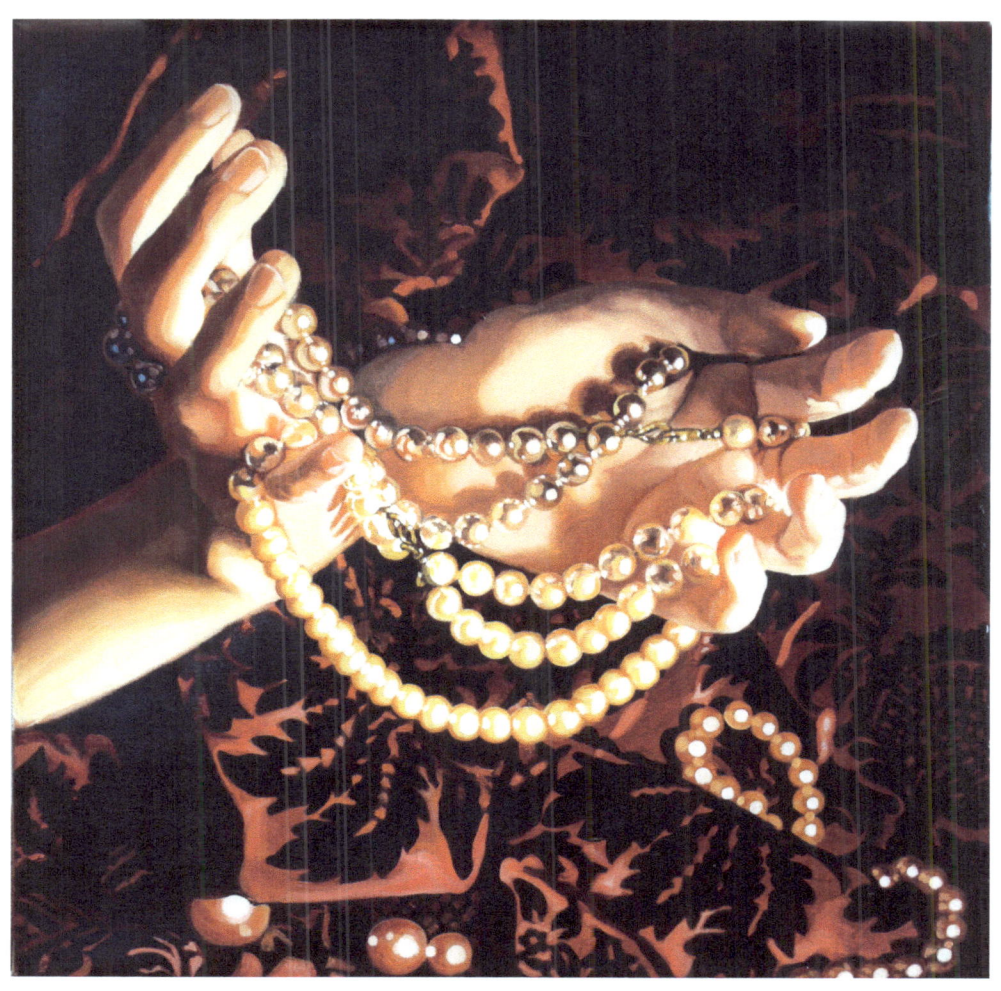

Lisa Ficarelli-Halpern, *Baroque Red,* oil on canvas, 2012, 14 x 14 inches

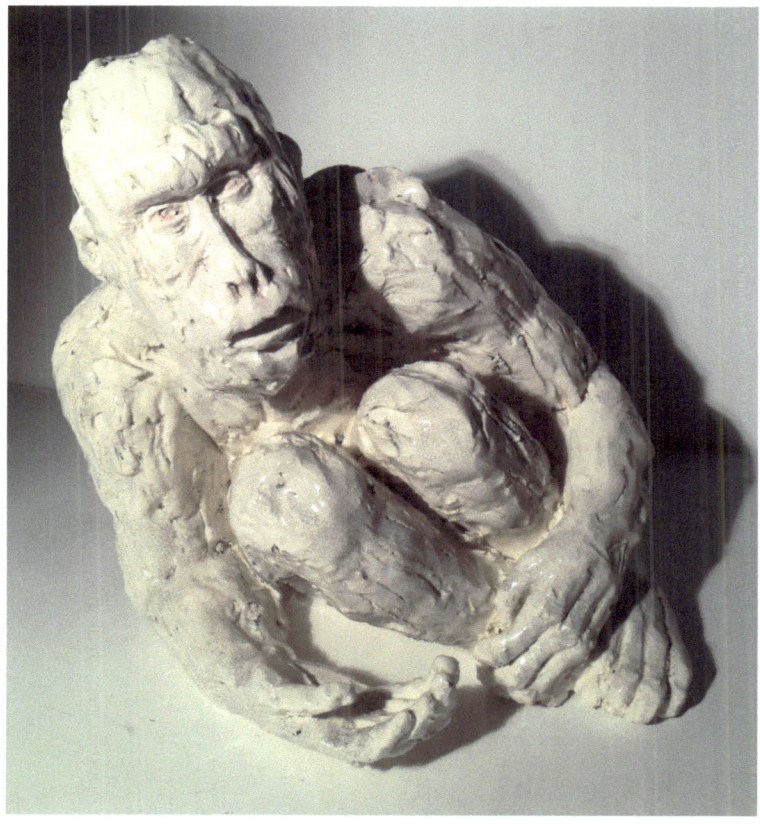

Dasha Bazanova, Monkey Asking Porcelain , 2014

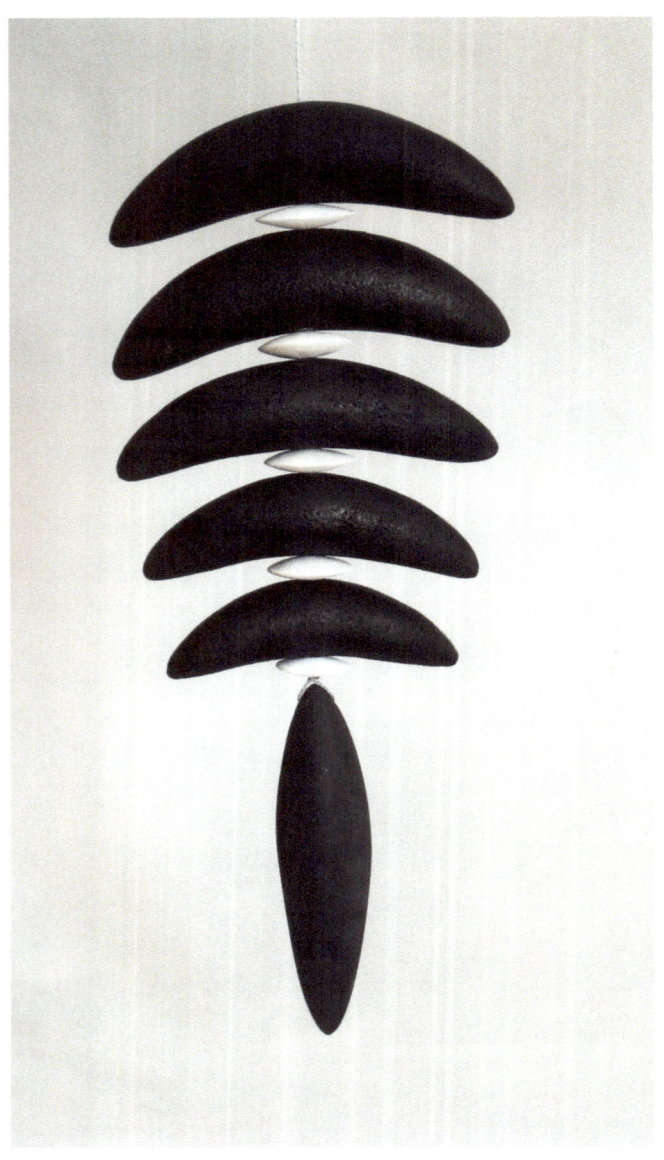

Helena Starcevic, Hanging Rachis-Long Tail, 2013 21 x 10 x 3 inches

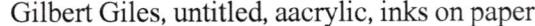
Gilbert Giles, untitled, aacrylic, inks on paper

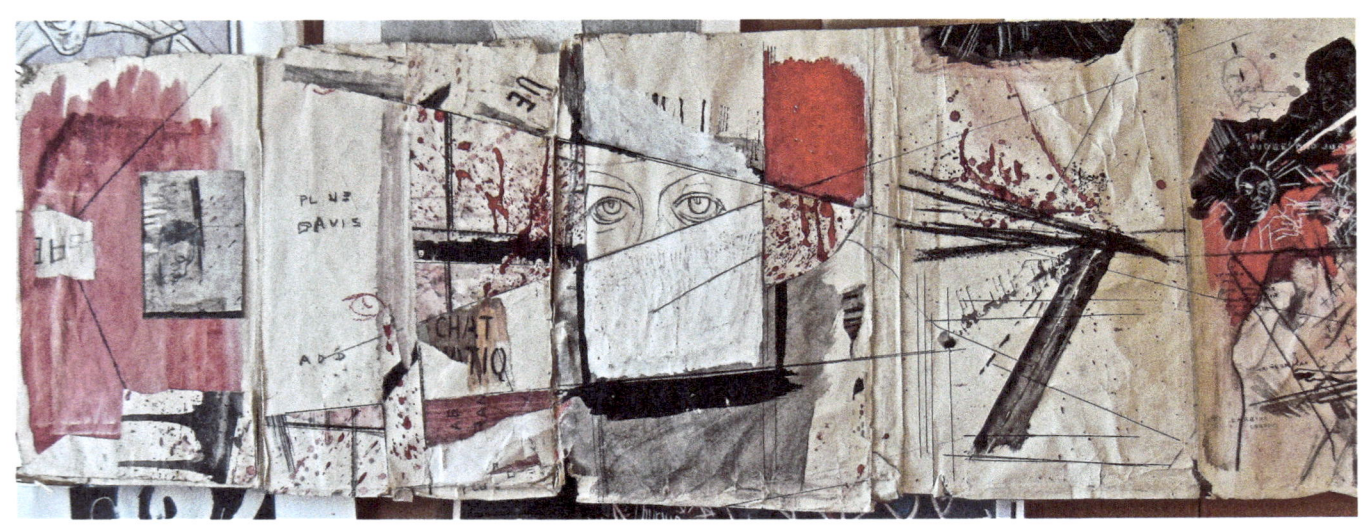

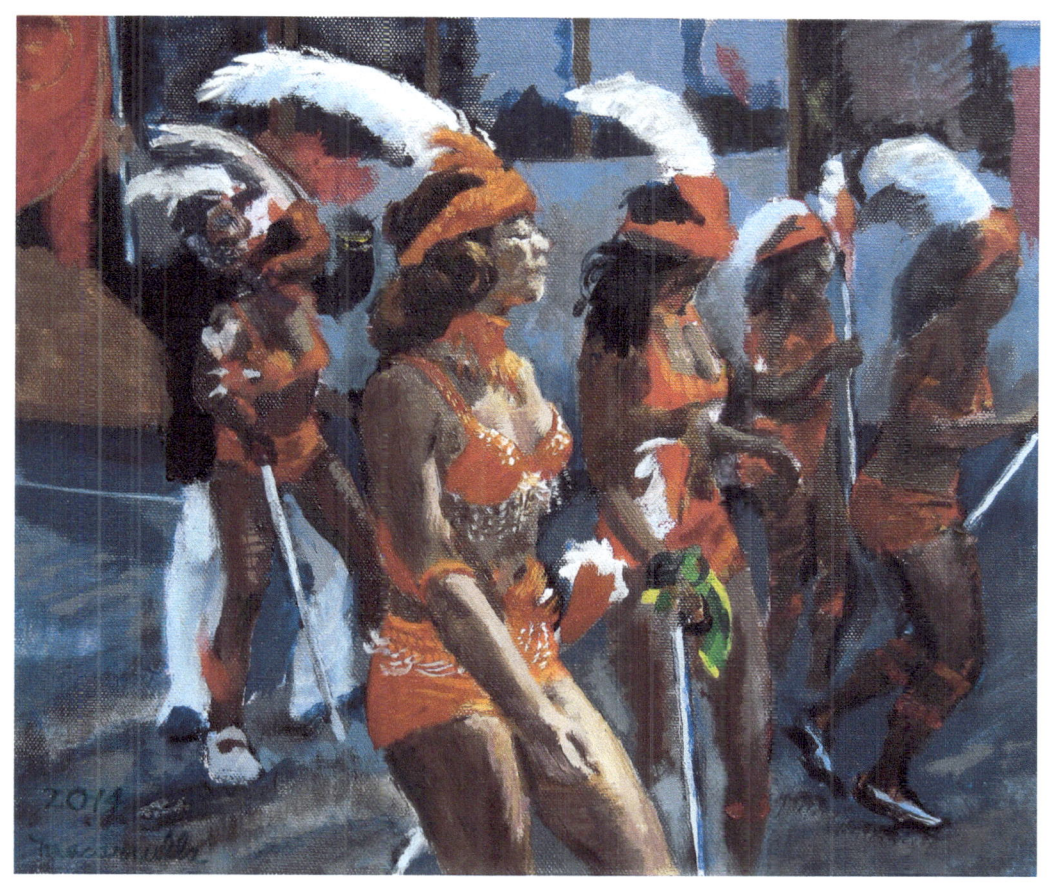

Manuel Macarrulla, Orange Ladies, 2014; Oil on canvas; 10 3/4 X 12 3/4 inches

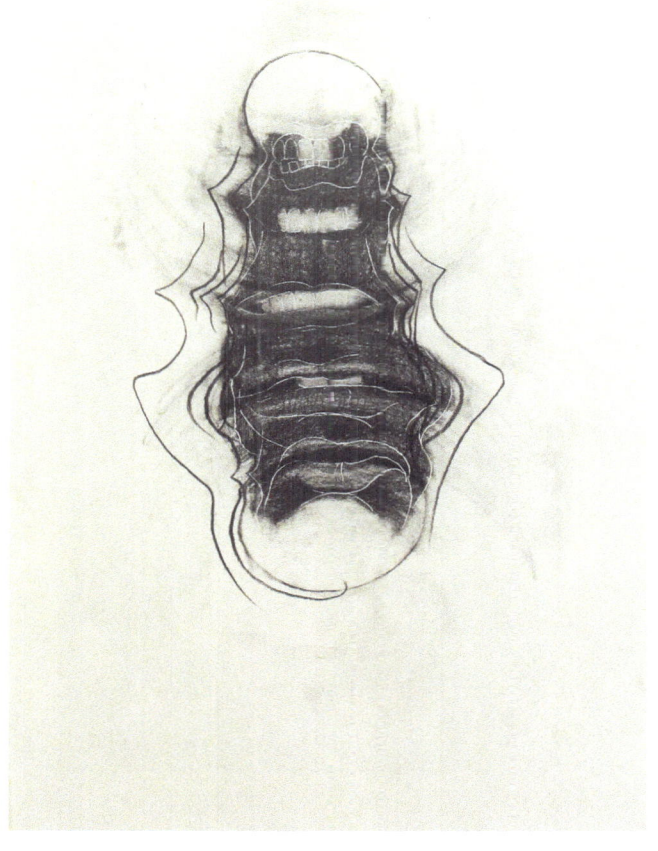

Joanne Howard, Totem Pencil/Paper 18″ x 15″ 2014

Alan Walker, Wayne's World, acryilic on canvas, 2014

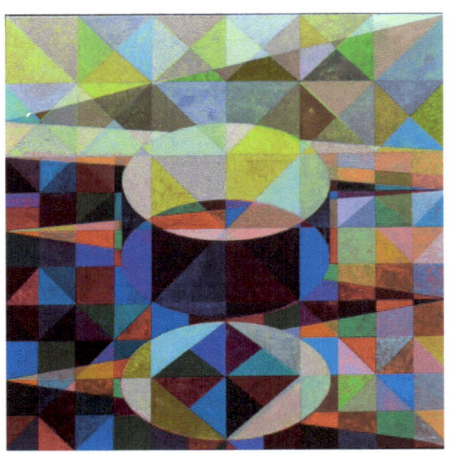

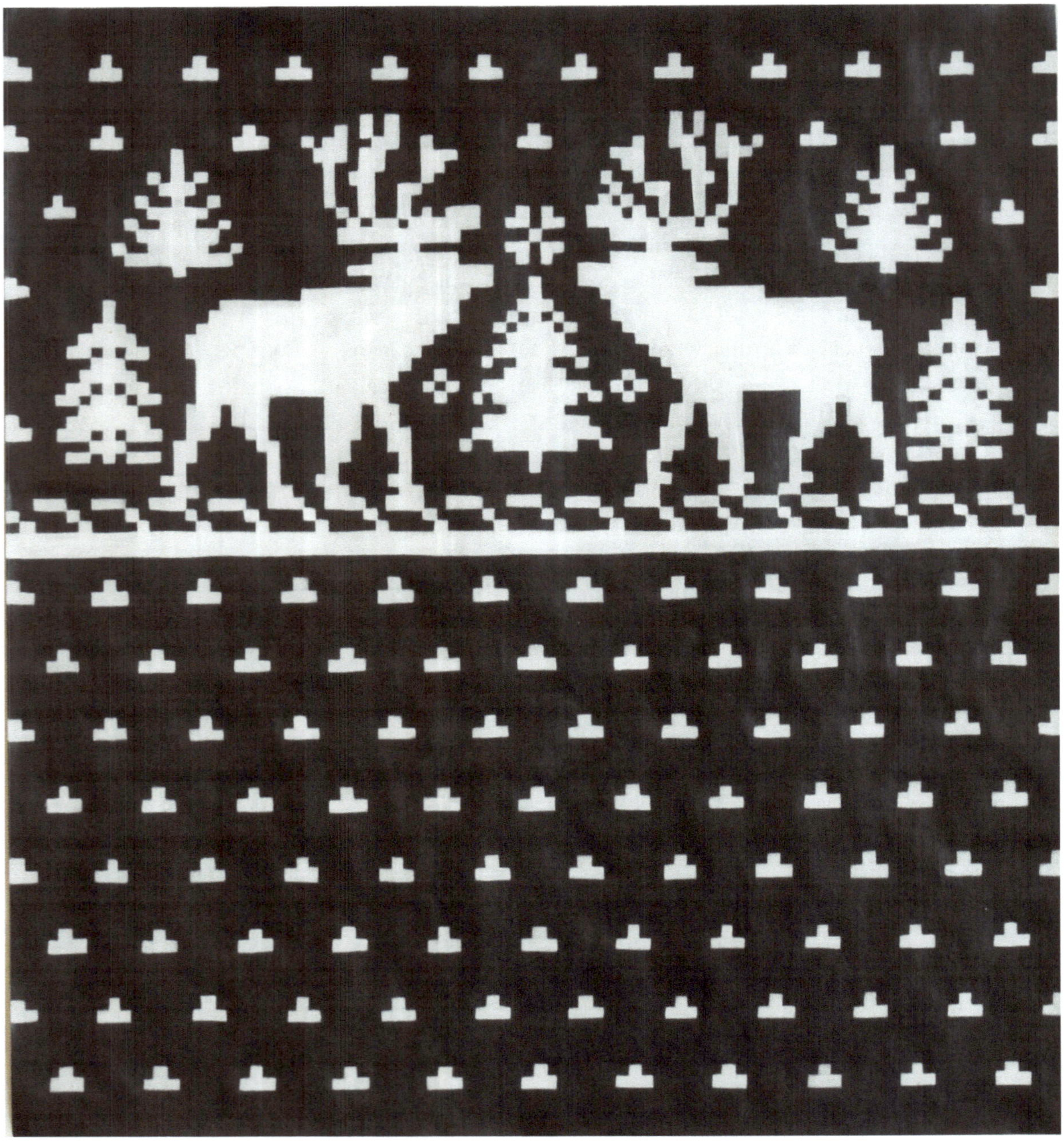

Seasonal Sweater, 2011, acrylic enamel paint on paper, 24 x 22 inches

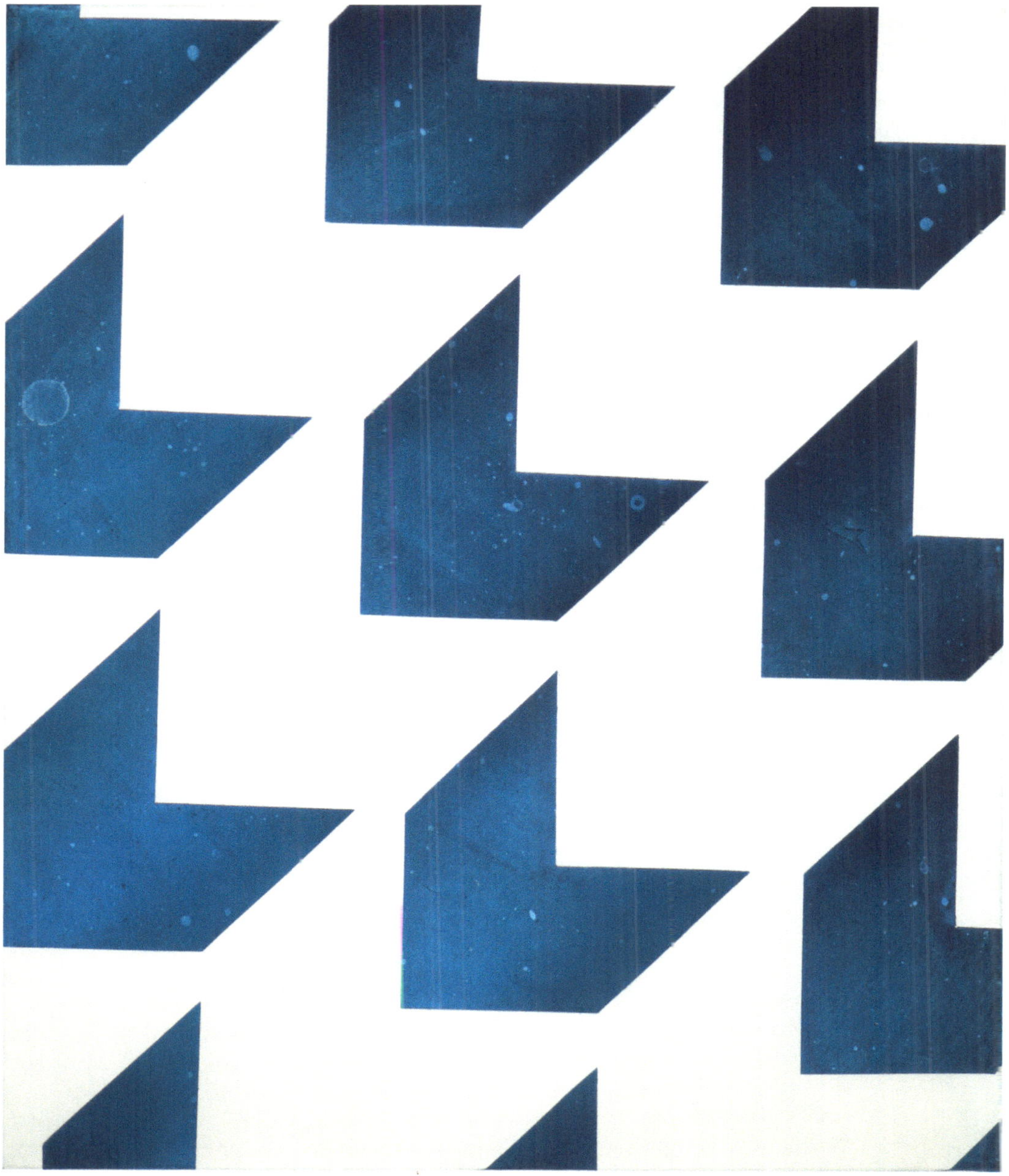

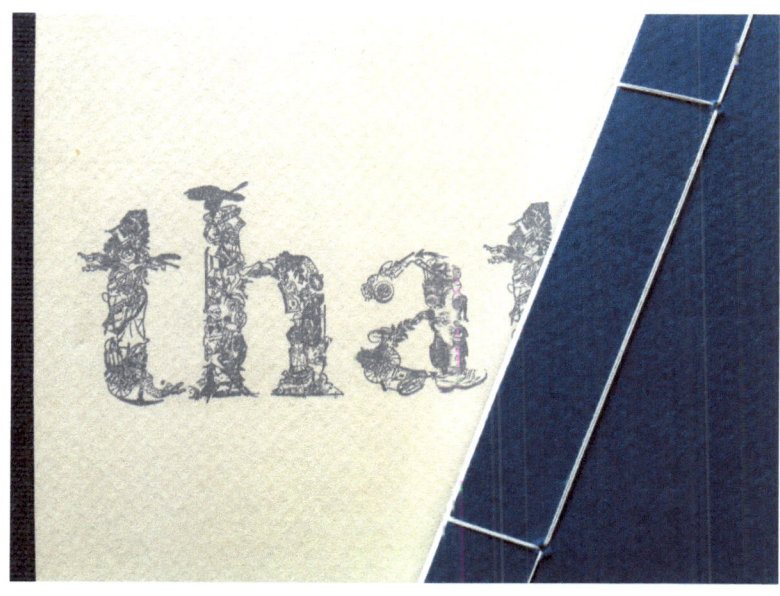

Enrico Gomez, Eventide, 2013, acrylic on stretched paper, 12x10

Peter Duffin,
Libertad, 2013 10 x 13 inchhes

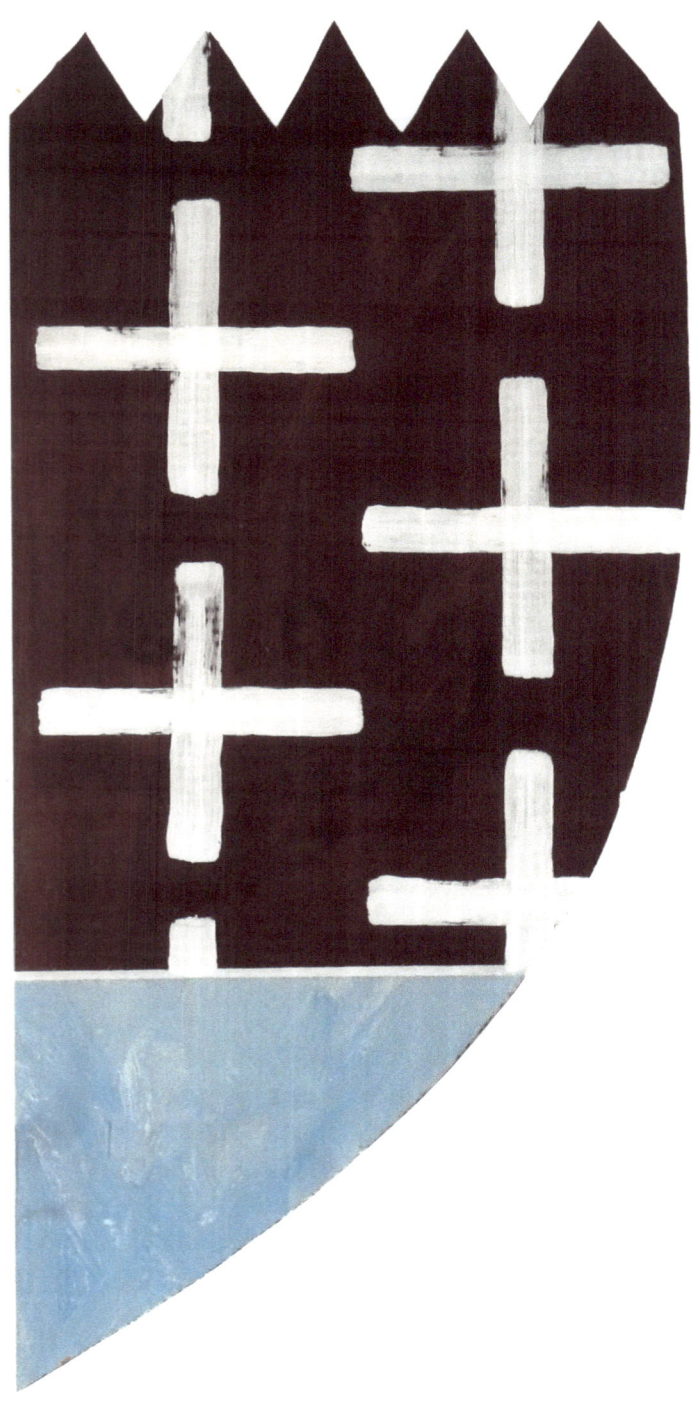

Vincent Romaniello, Double Crosses
35 x 16.5 inches, acrylic paint on found cardboard

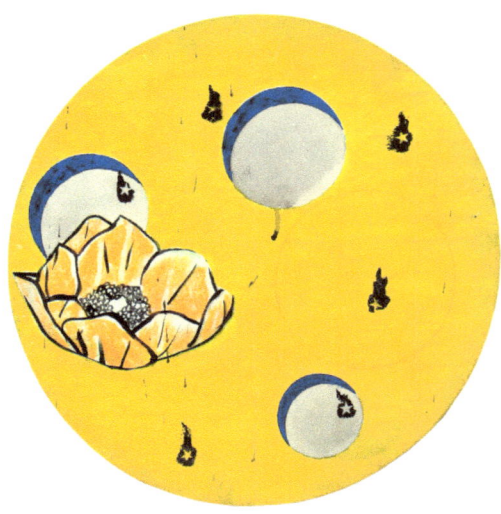

Greg Brickey, Yellow Circle, acrylic on canvas

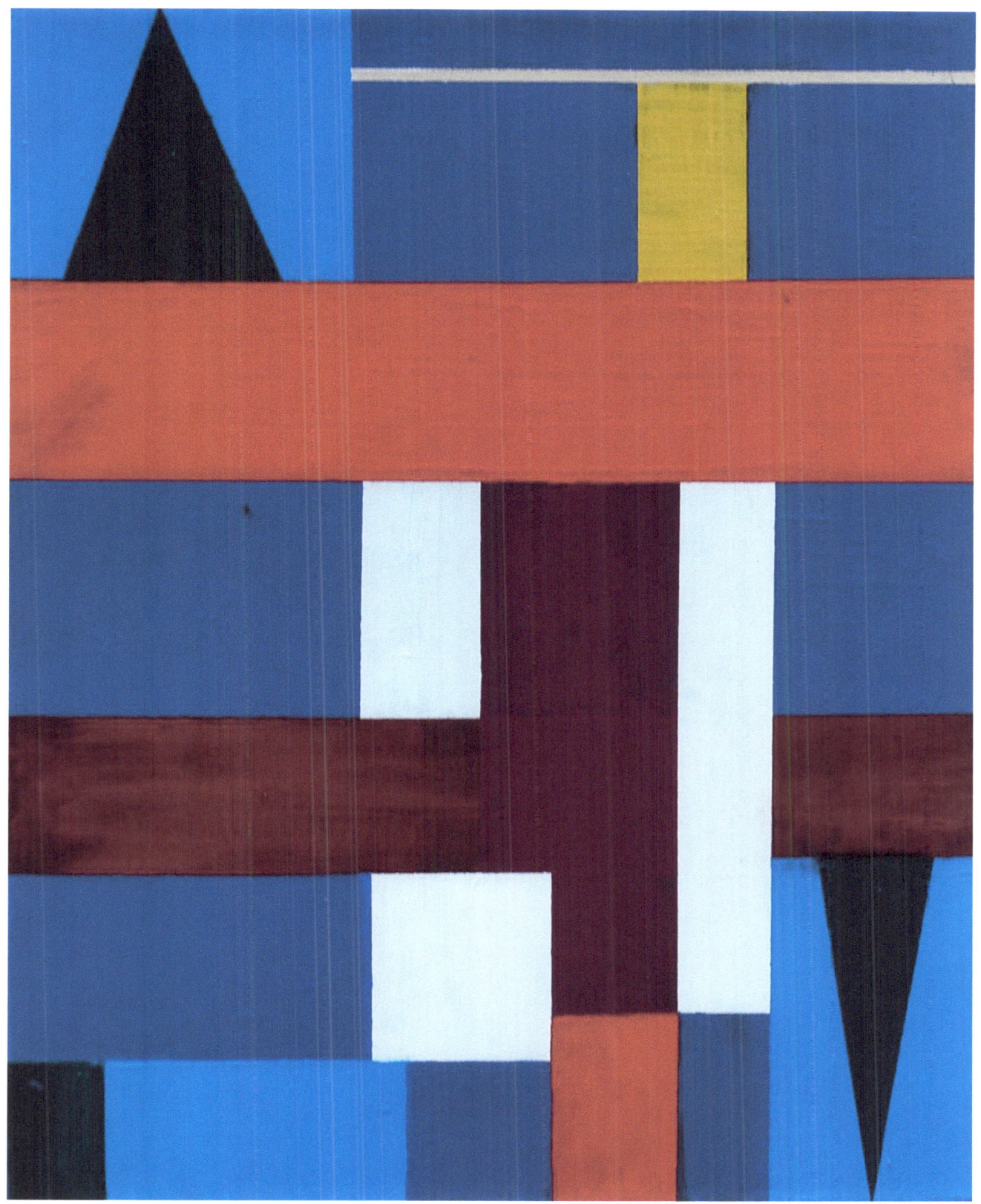

Eveline Luppi, ColorSignal 2, 2011 16 x 20 inches

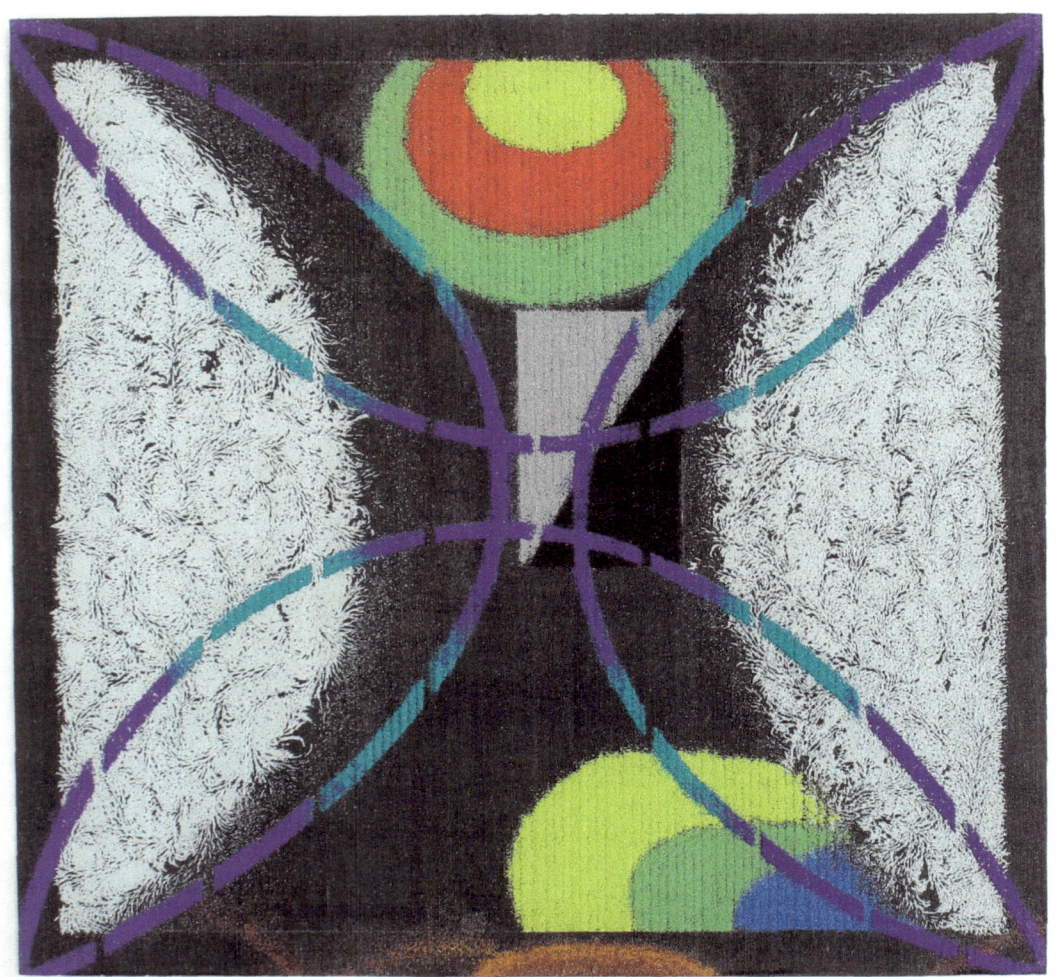

Ryan DaWalt, Lens Swell 3, 23 x 23 inches Hand-made pigments cast in magnetic fields on linen on board 2013

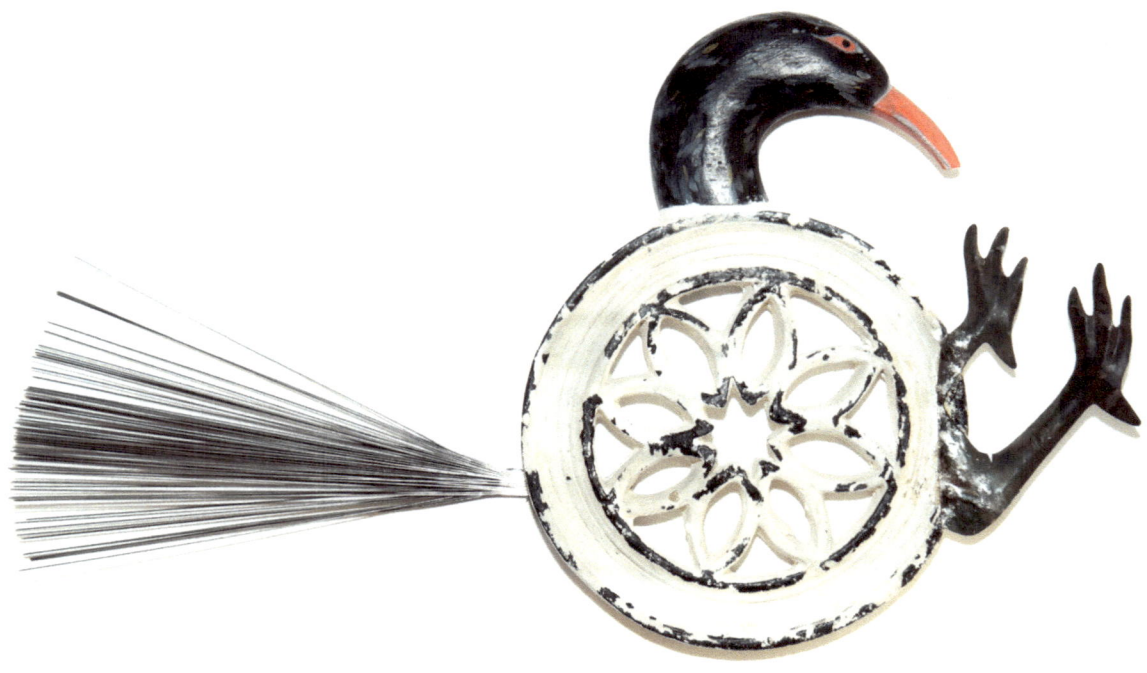

Jodie Fink, Bird, 2013 7 1/4 x 12 3/4 x 1 inches

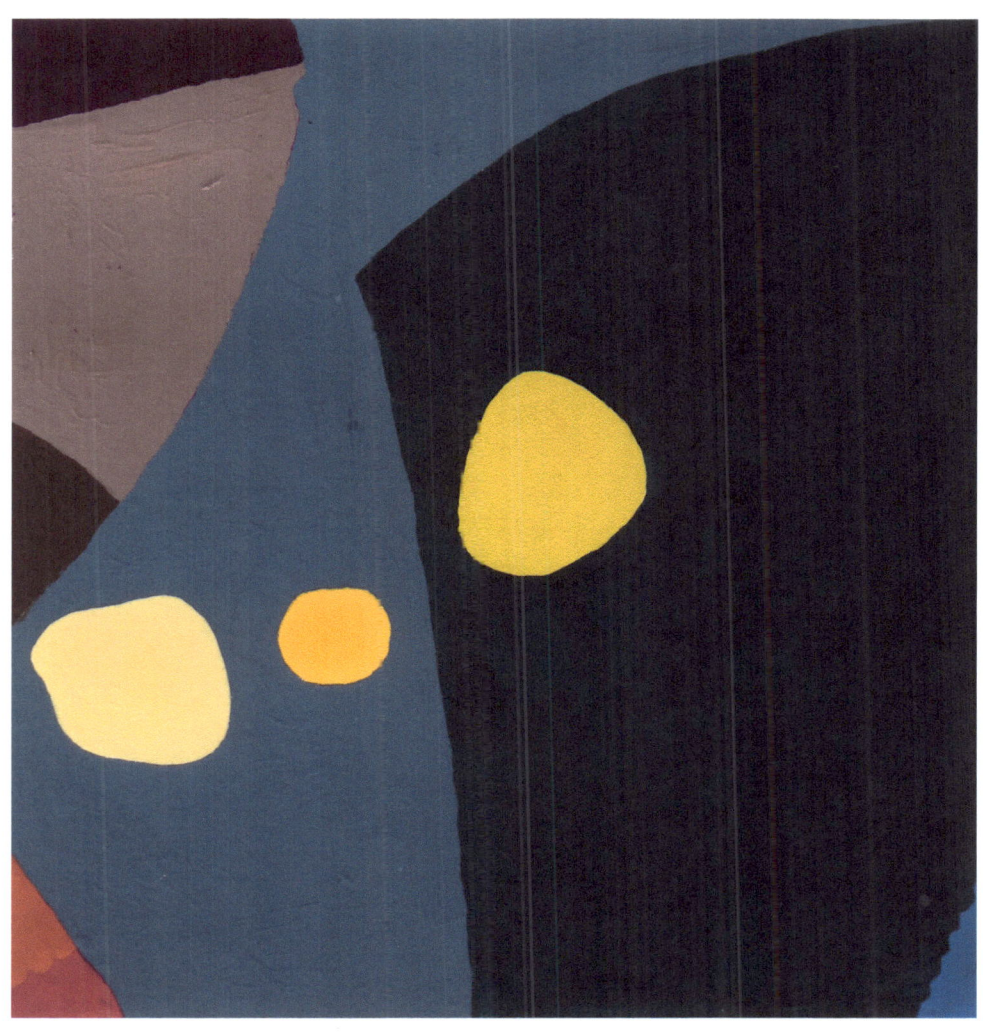

Barbara Marks, yellow 3
8.25 × 8.25 inches, acrylic-gouache and graphite on paper

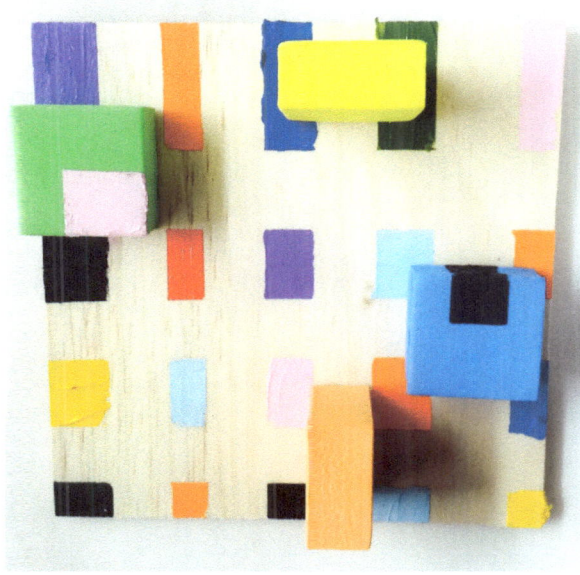

Suzan Shutan, Untitled , mixed media

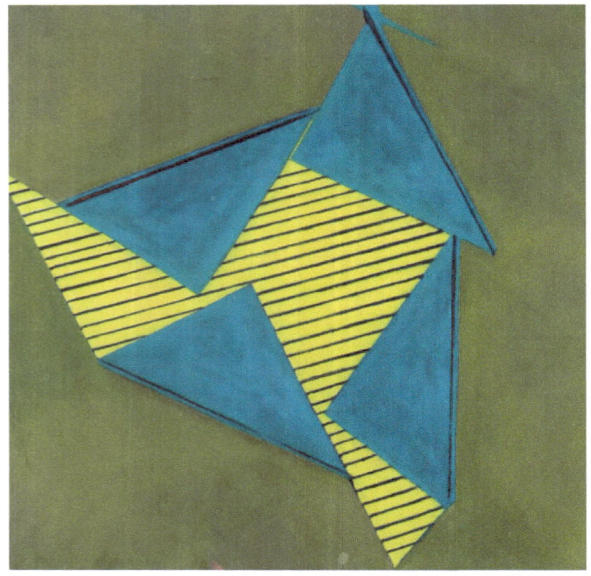

FranShalom, Triangulate, 2012 12 x 12 inches

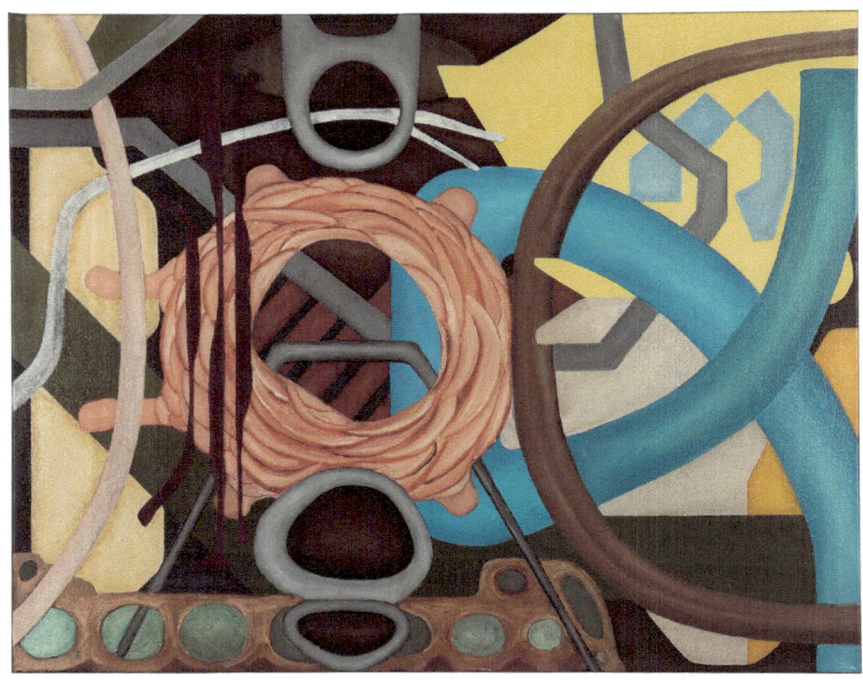

Greg Letson-High Noon, 2014, 30 x 24 inches

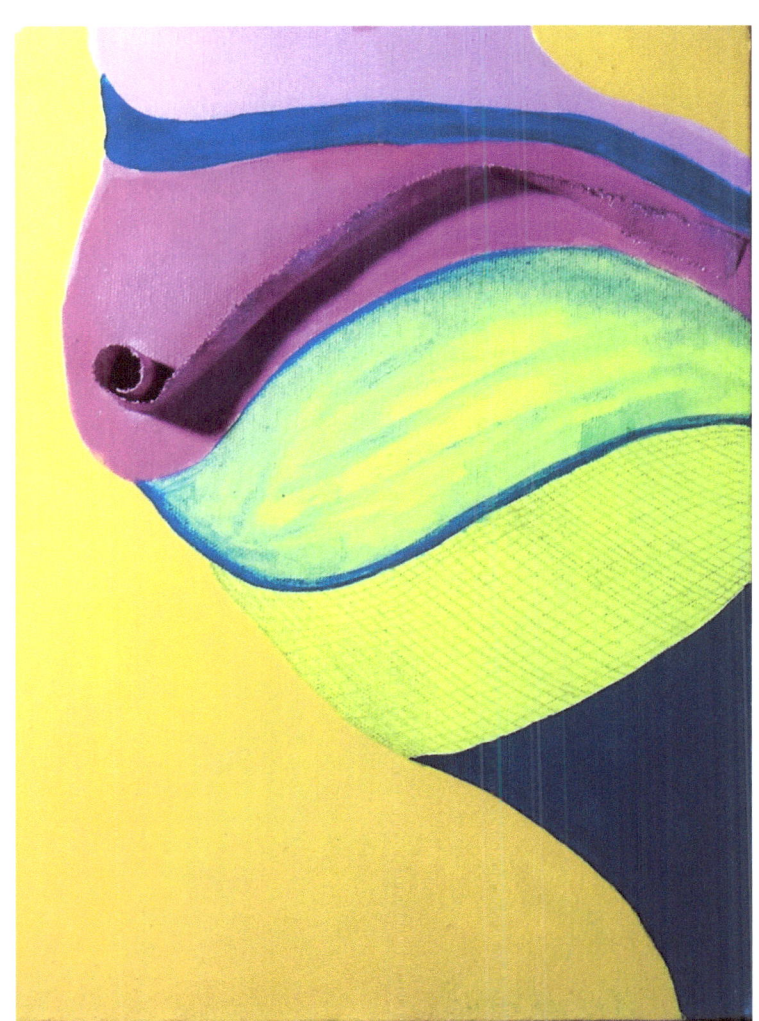

Caridad Kenned, The Wave 2., 2013. 12 x 9 inches

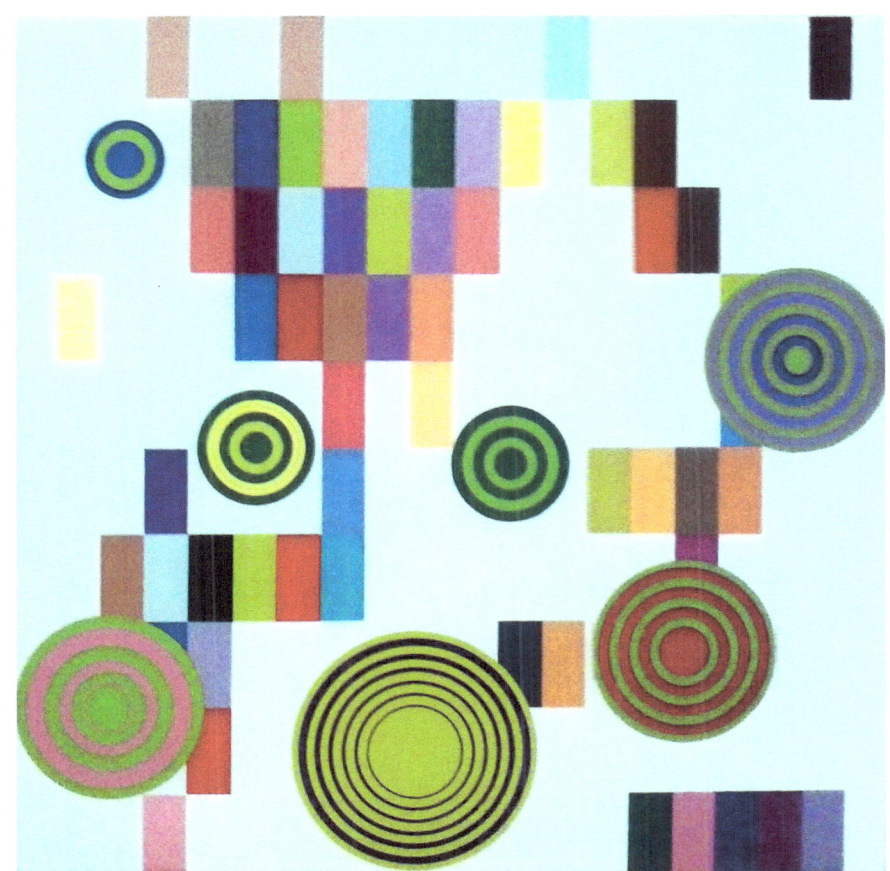

Peter Bill, Acrylic n canvas 2014

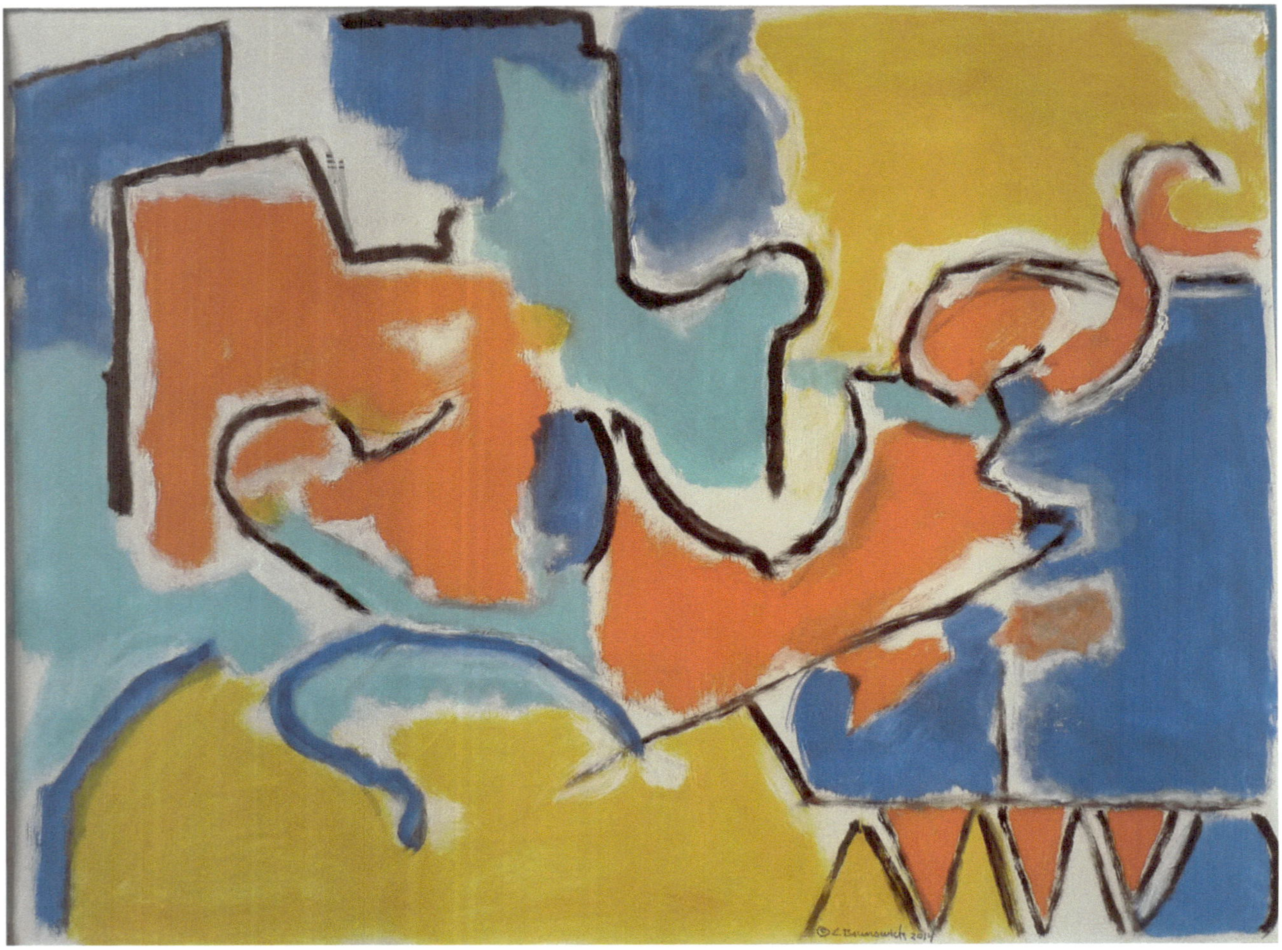

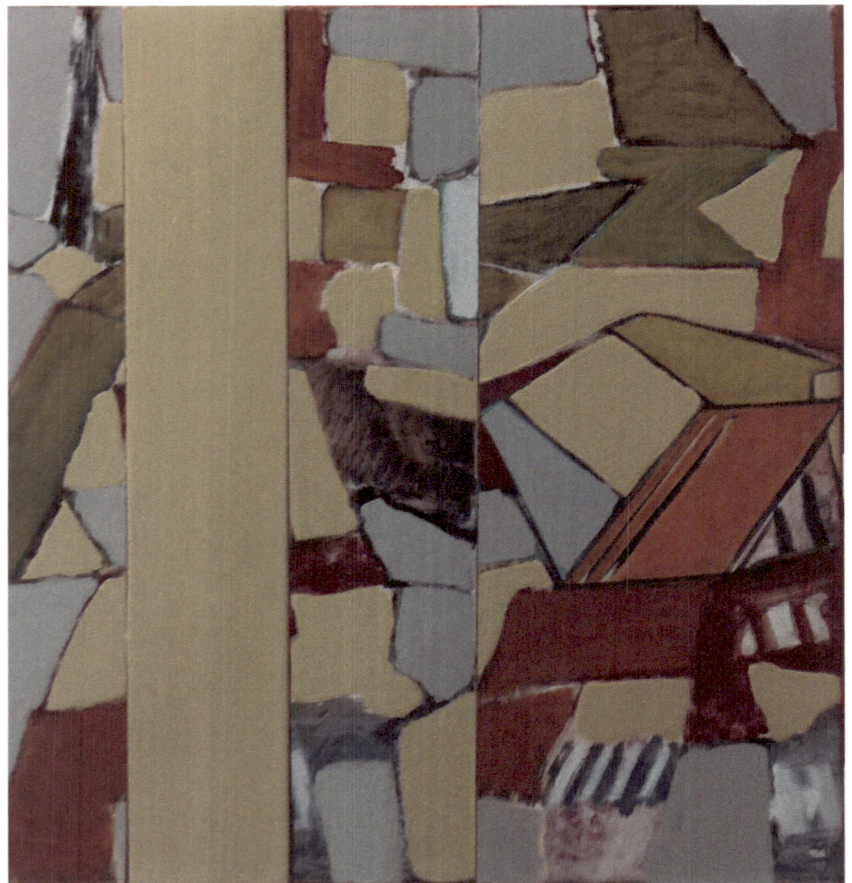

Cecile Brunswick, OfftheHook 2012 18-x24 OilonPanel 2012

Ian Mack, untitled, oil on board,
24 x 18 inches

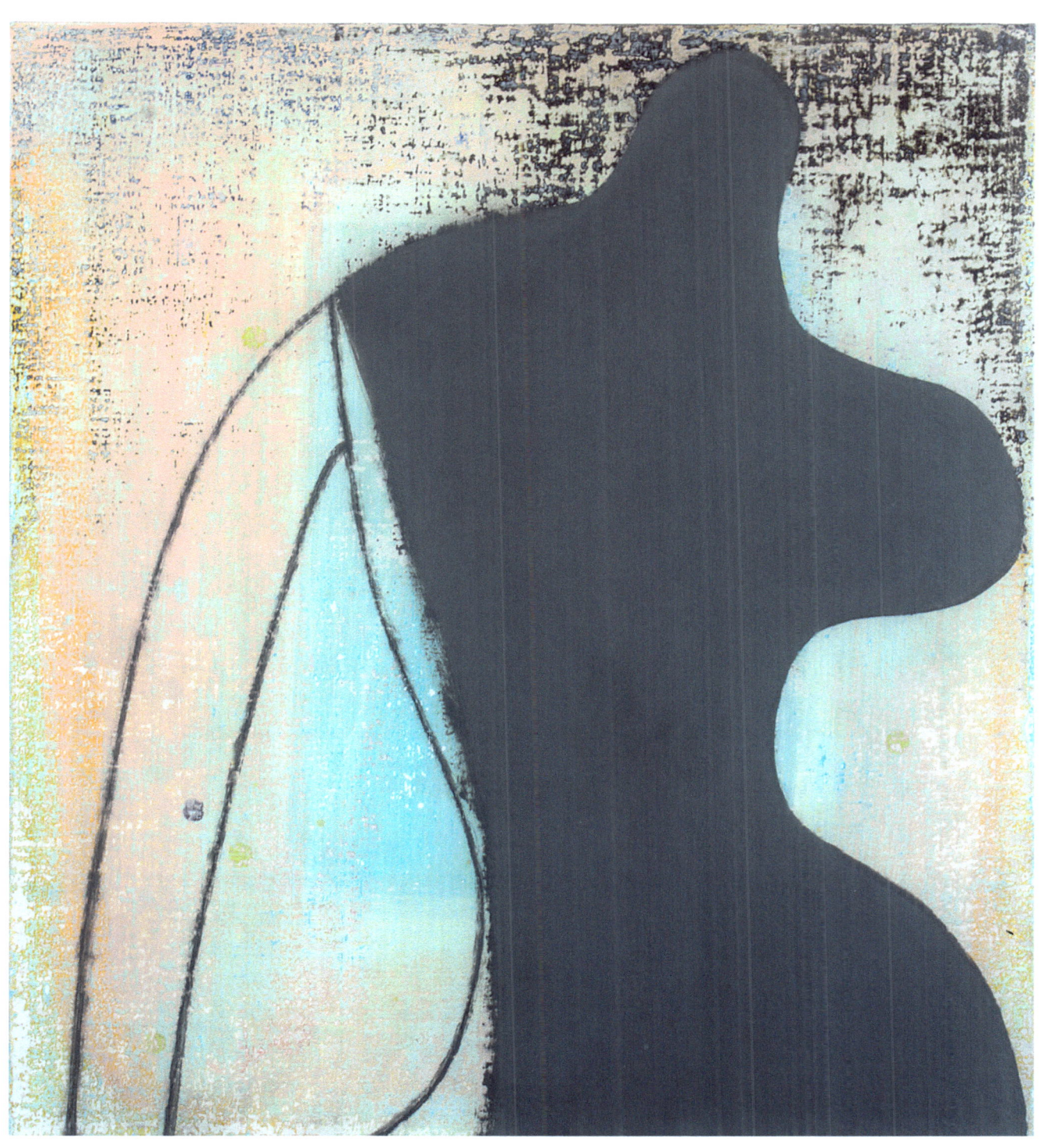

Patricia Satterlee, Gloria, 07-2012 26 x 23.5 inches

KevinMcCaffrey, Study in Blue-Green, 2014 19.5 x 25.5 inches

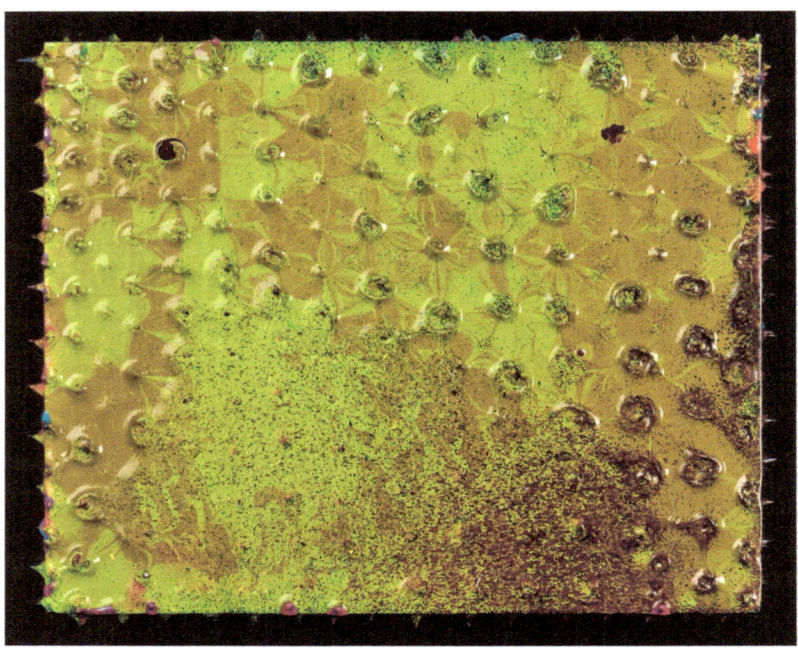

Ellen Hackl Fagan,   Paint, acrylic, latex, ink, enamel 8 x 10 x 3 inches

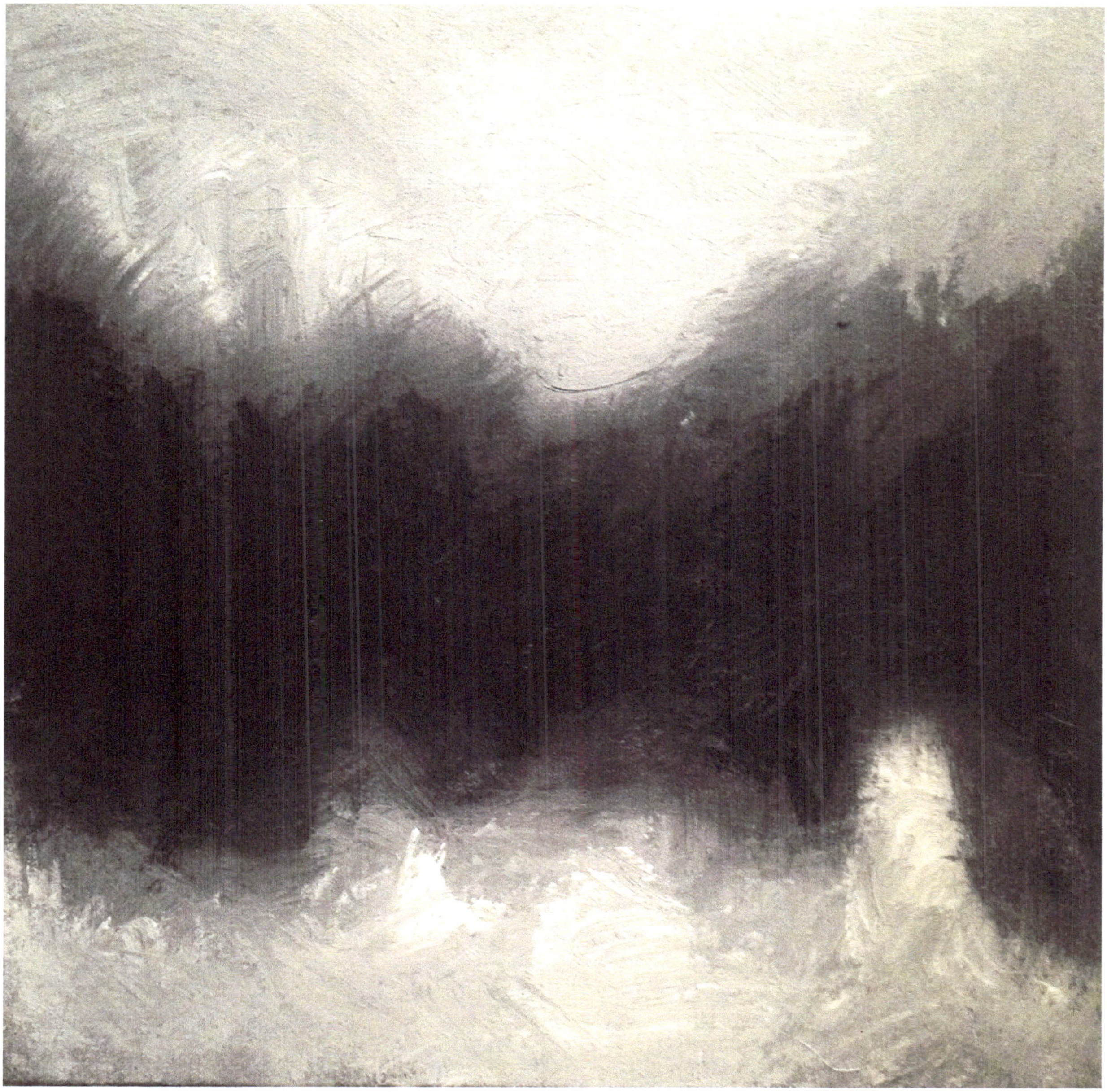

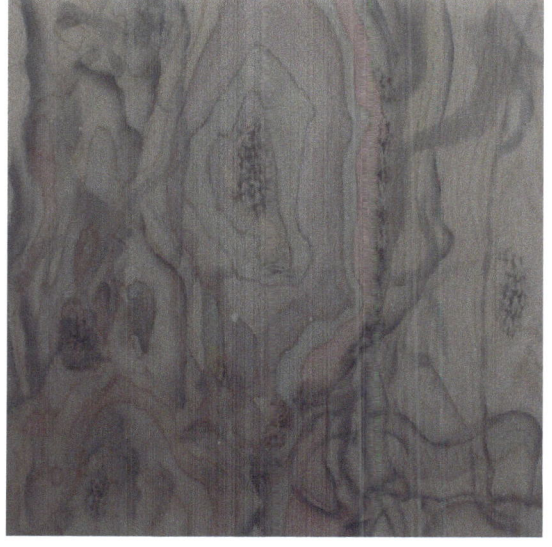

Heidi Curko, Black and White #1

Robyn Ellenbogen, Always Close
16 x 16 inches, stainless steel wool, silverpoint
acrylic on birch panel with transparent gesso

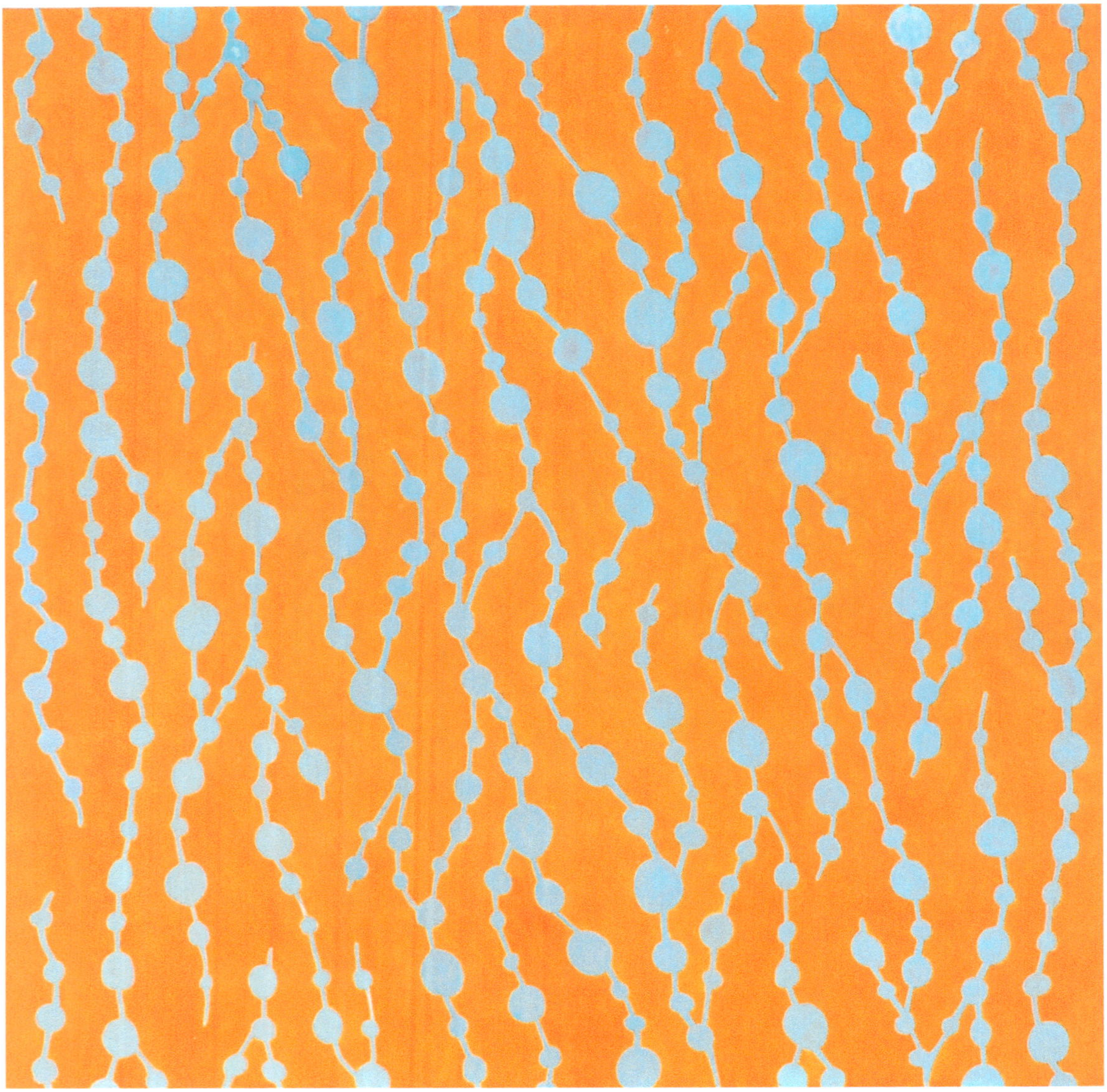

Dana Kane, Untitled   22 x 22 inches Acrylic & Gouache 2013

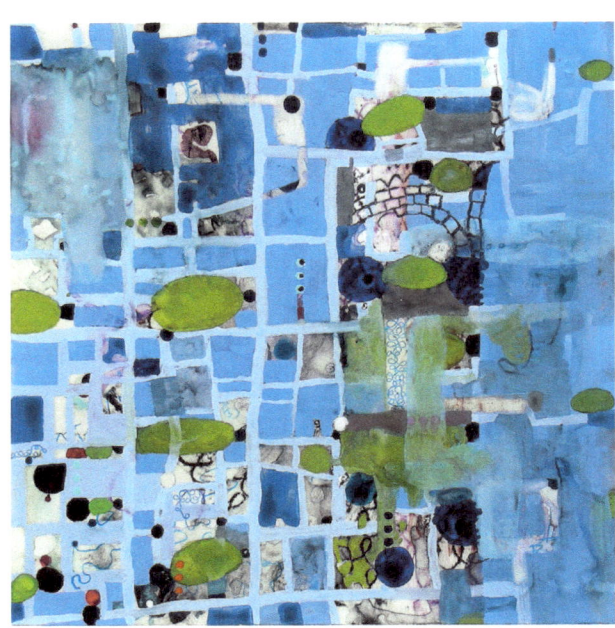

Untitled (5-2-13)
gouache, watercolor, ink on paper (yupo) paper
9" x 9"size of artwork (framed)

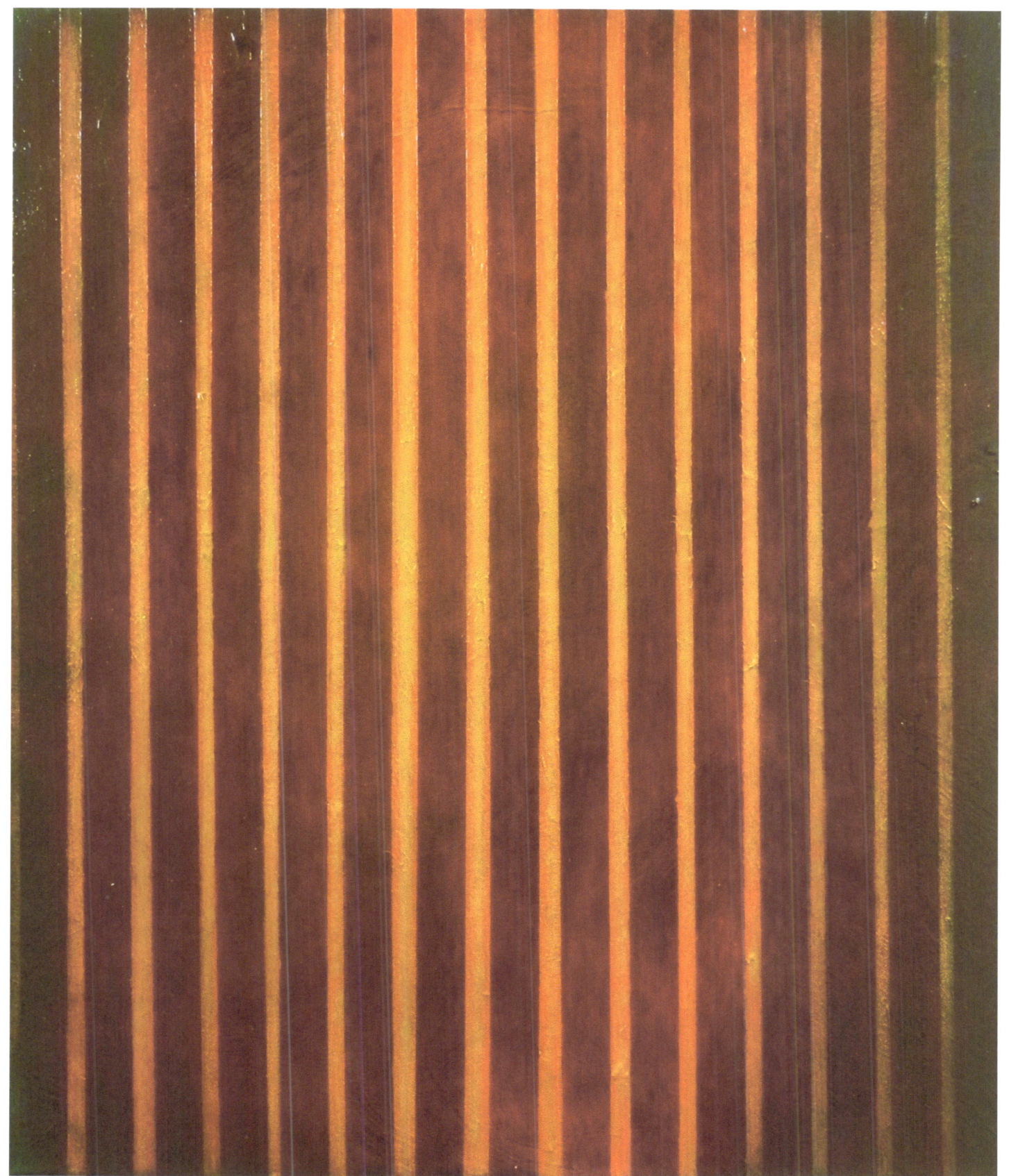

WilliamS⁻amos - Continuum lll-2014, 14 x 20 inches

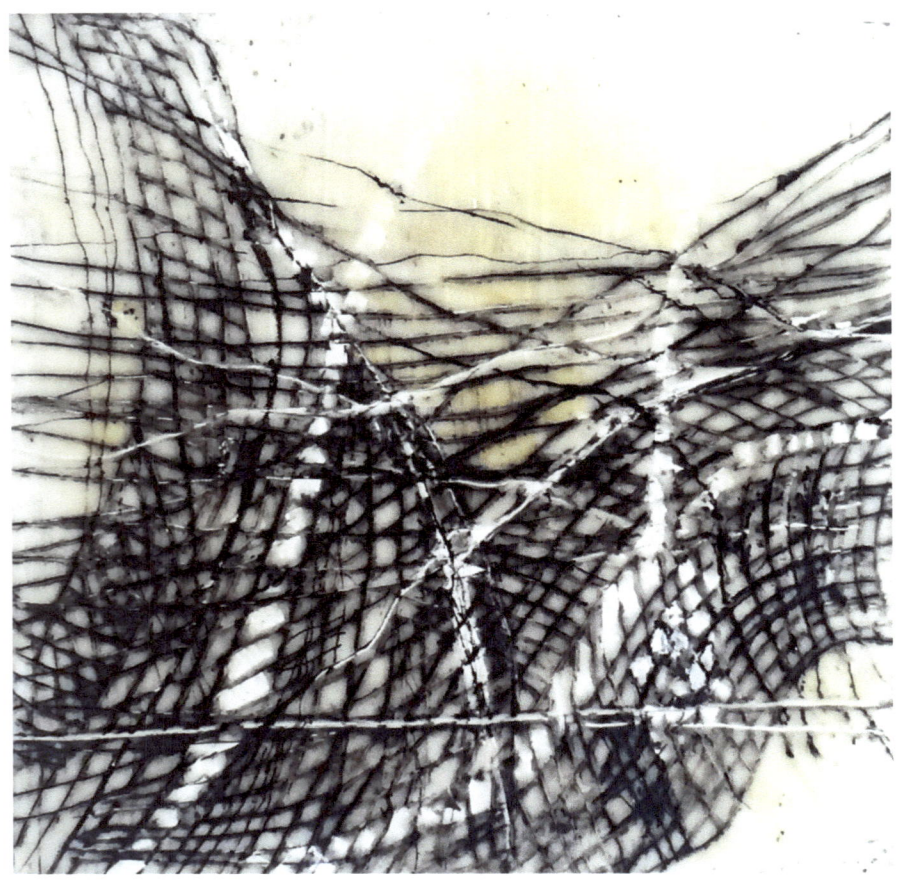

Megan Klim, Incision #1ink, oil, shellac on beeswax on wood 8" x 8" 2014

Austin Thomas
Wednesday (daily drawings)
(sometimes done over a couple of days)

2013 5X 3½ inches
Colored pencil on notebook cover

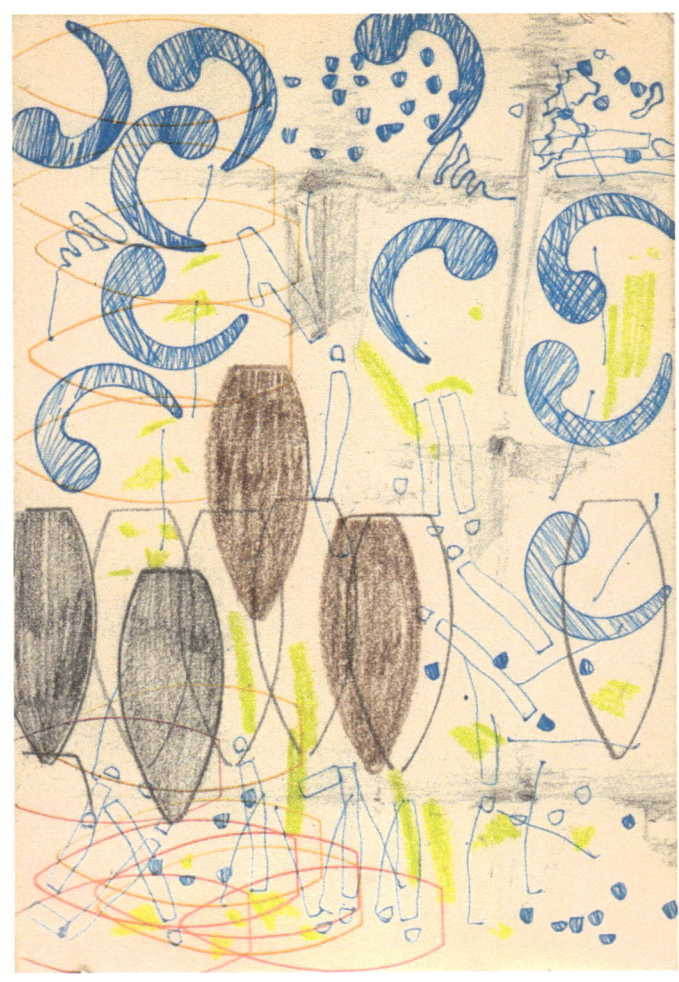

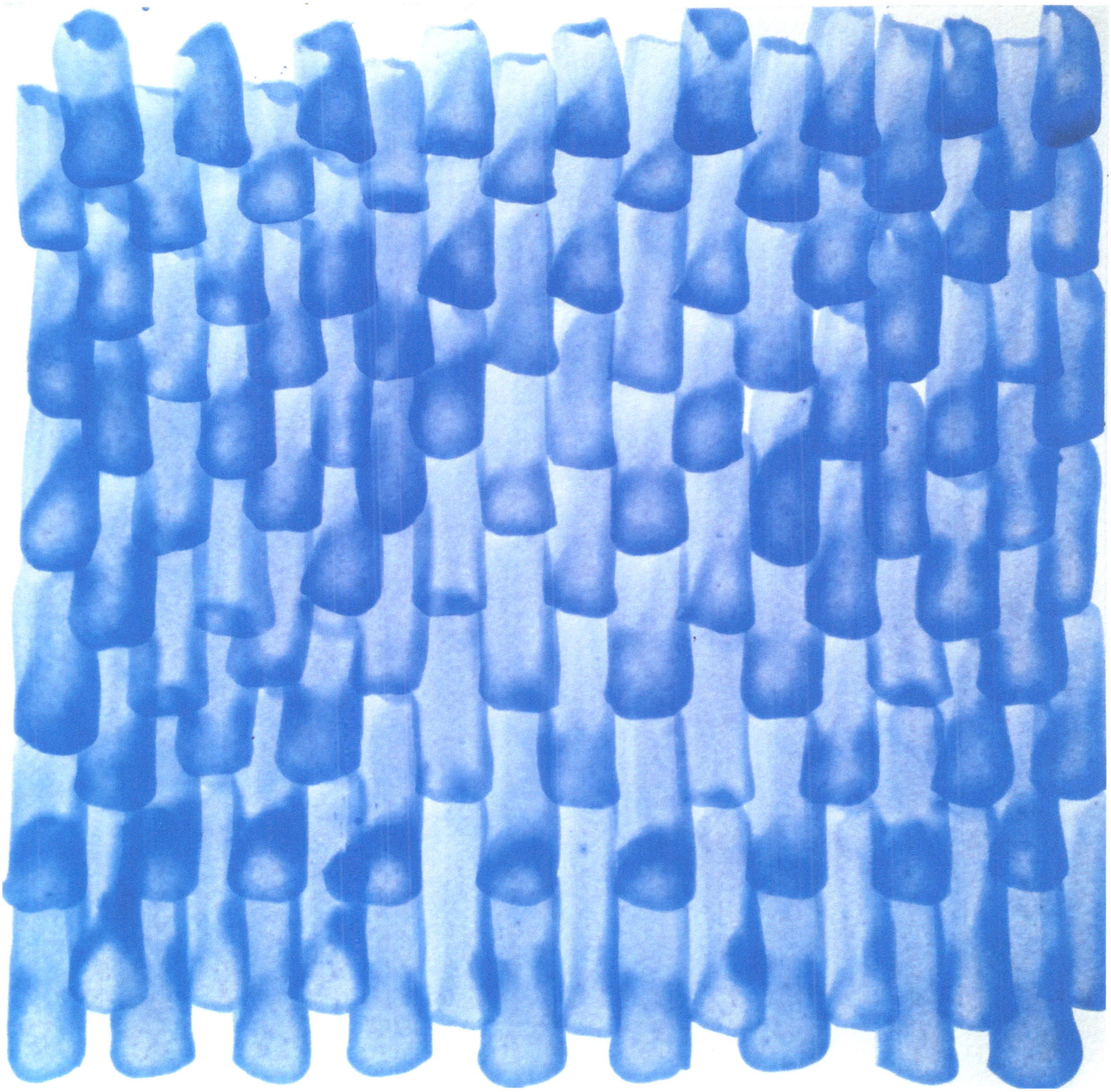

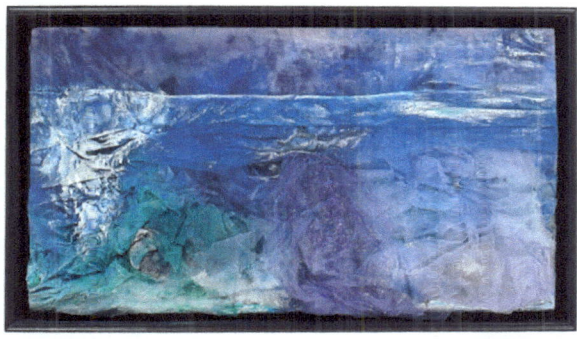

Ellie Murphy, Untitled (Falls), 2014, Encaustic on watercolor paper, 12″ x 12″

Alberte Bernier-Nature Bleue-2013-27x15 inches

Robin Feld   Looking Nowhere, 2014, oil on canvas, 12 x 12 inches

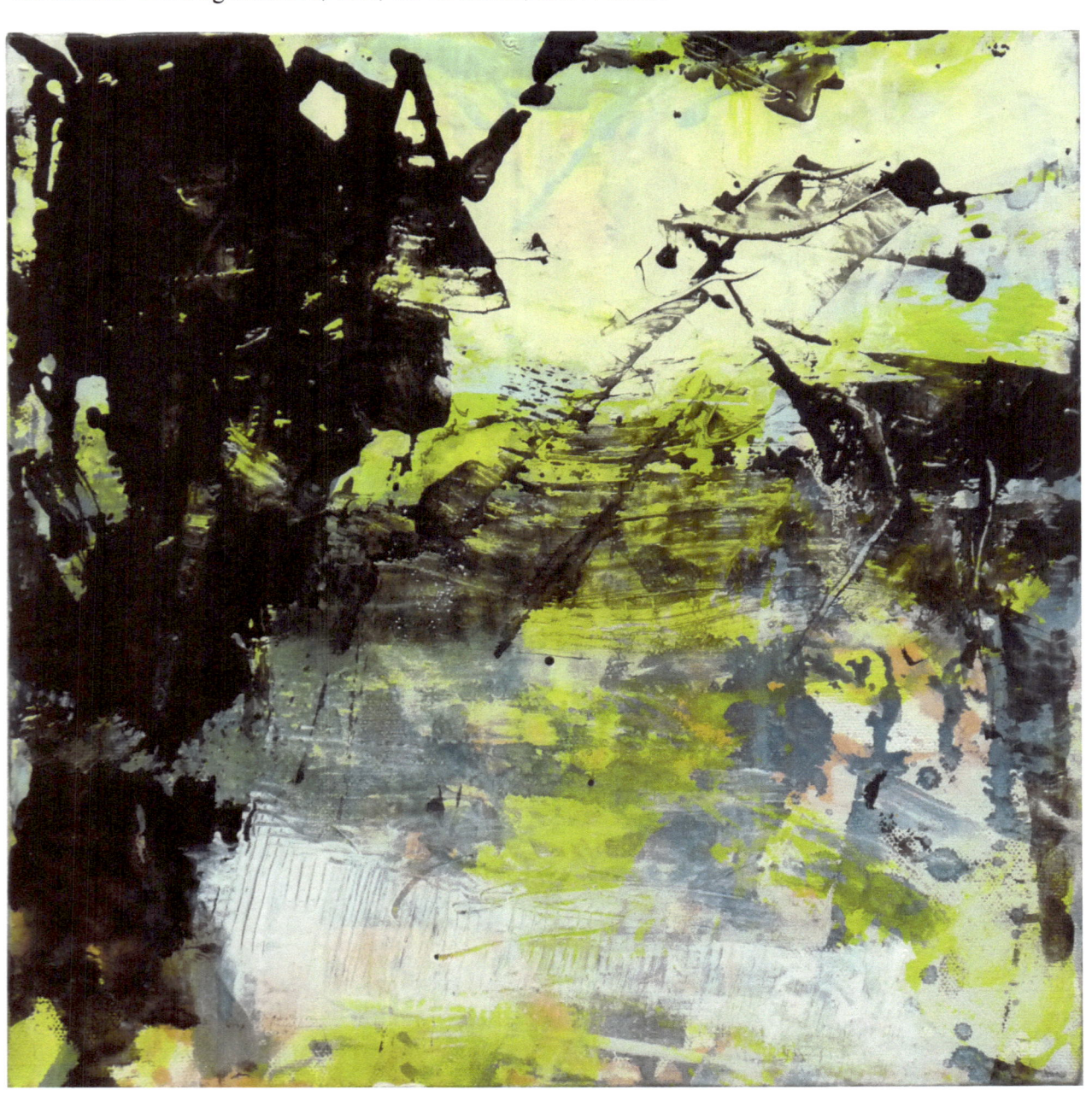

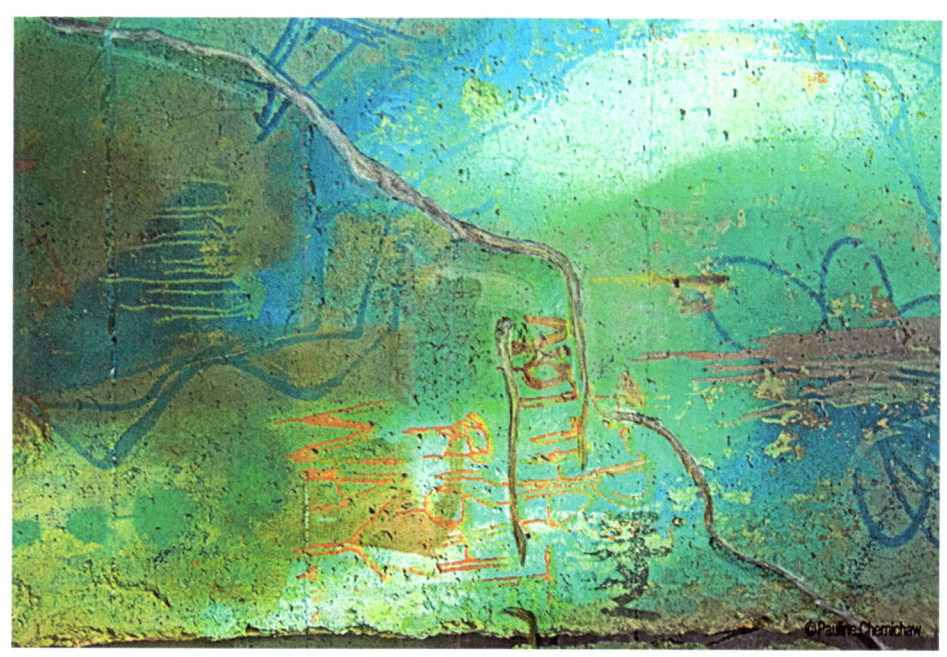

Pauline Chernichaw, Searching For Happiness 2014 22 X 28 inches framed

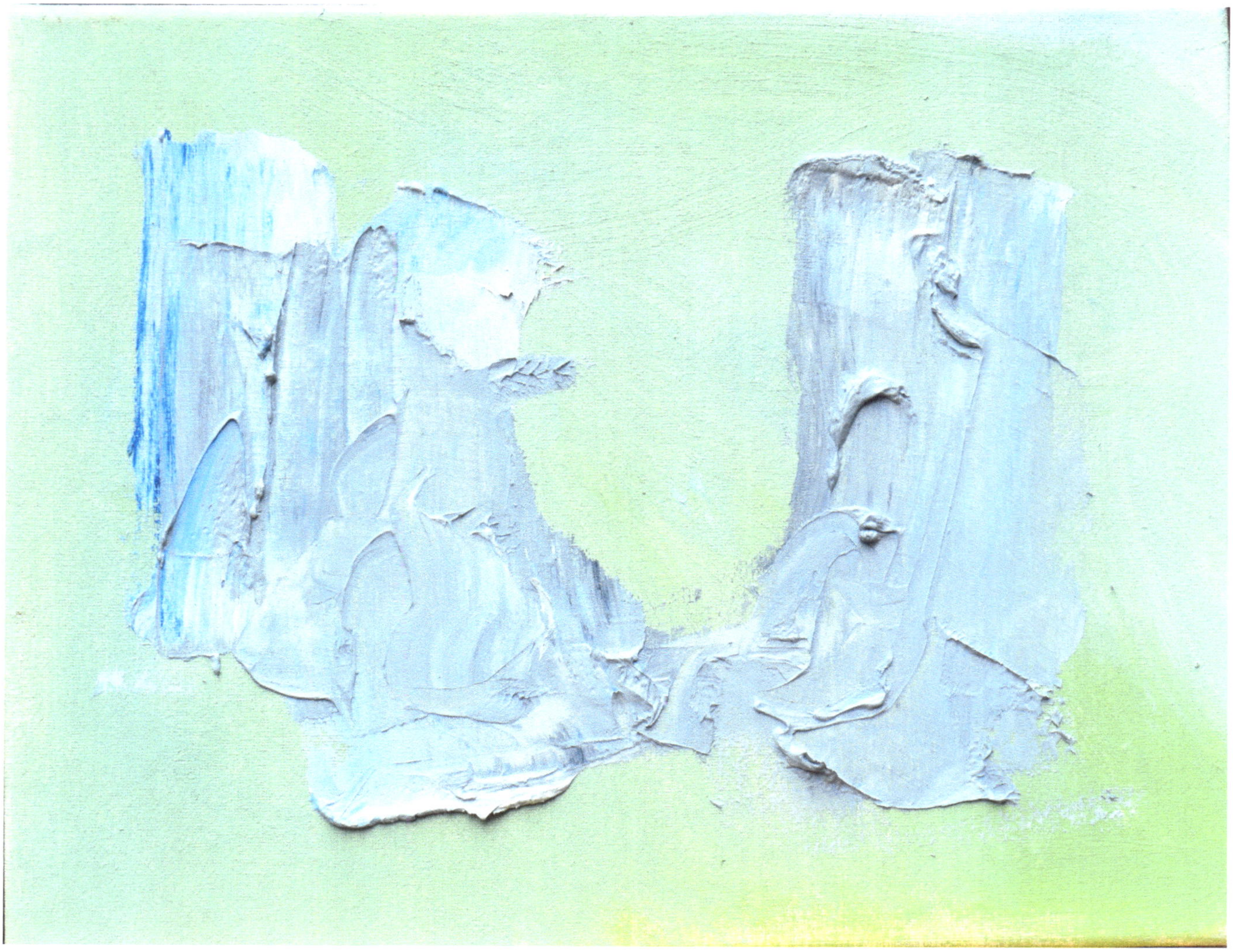

RichardWhite, History, 2 of 4, 2014, 14 x 11inches

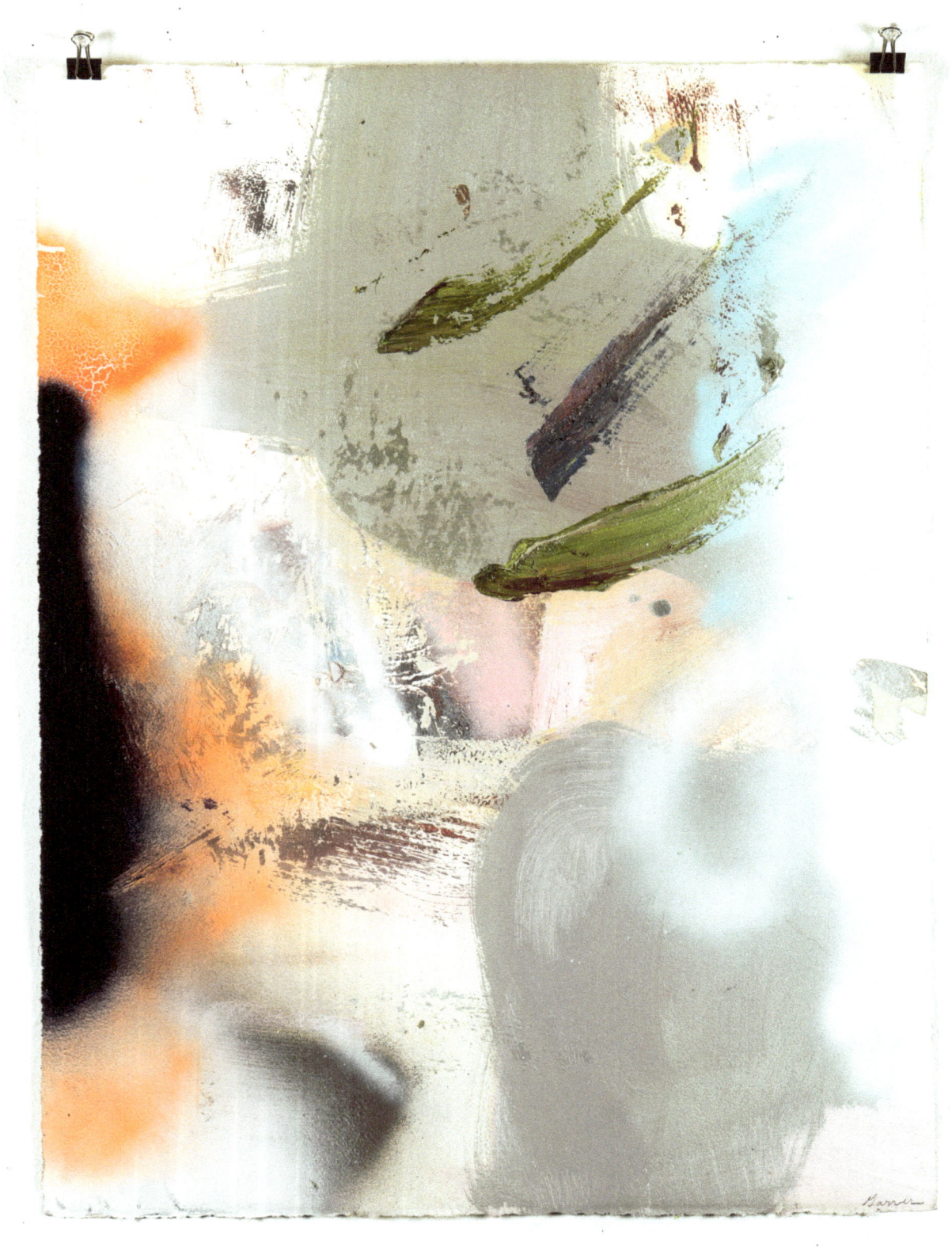

Glenn Garver, Untitled, 3, 2014, oil and spray paint on paper18 x 26 inches

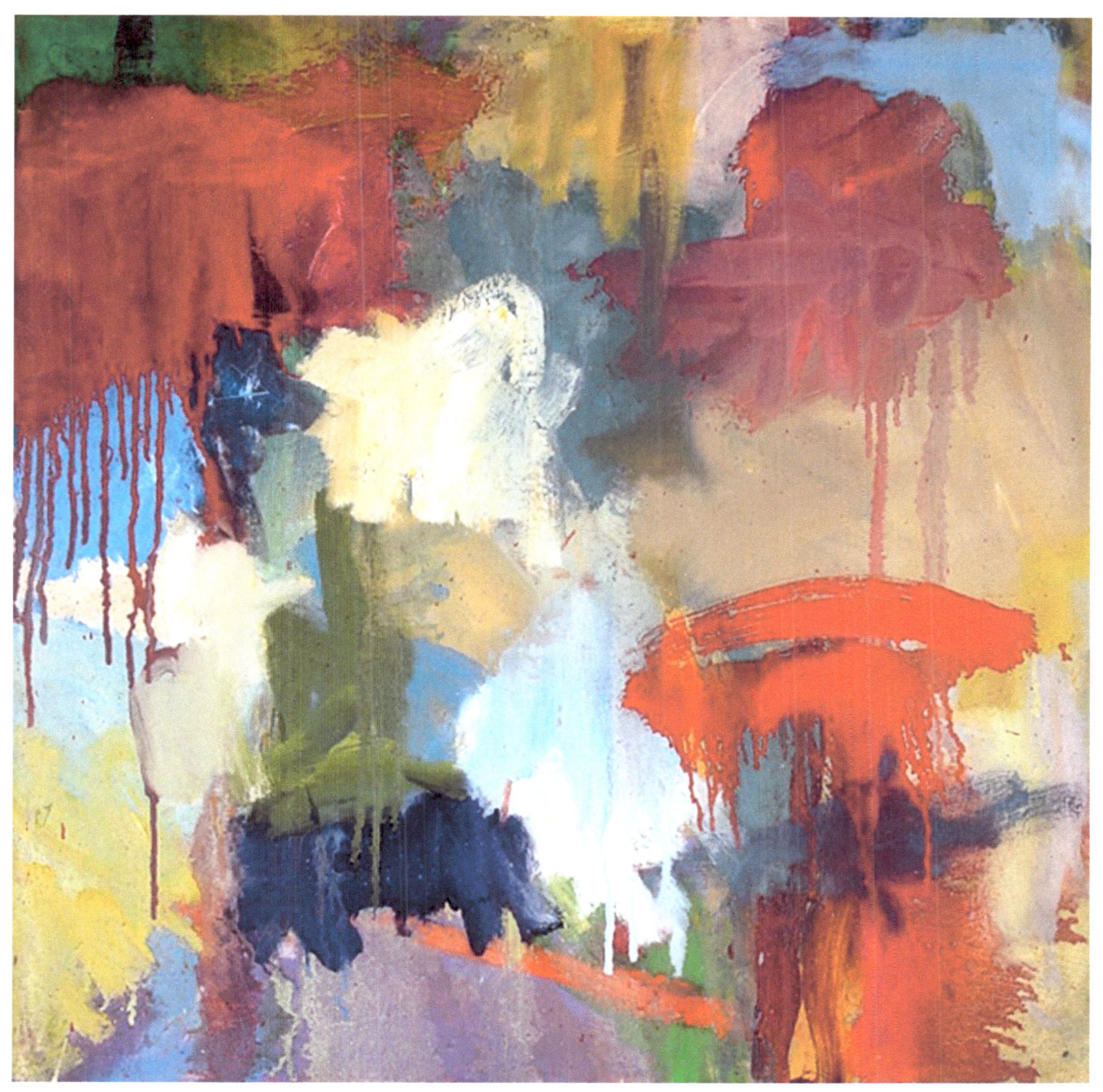

Marianne DeAngelis, give us a kiss 2014, oil on canvas, 24 x 24 in

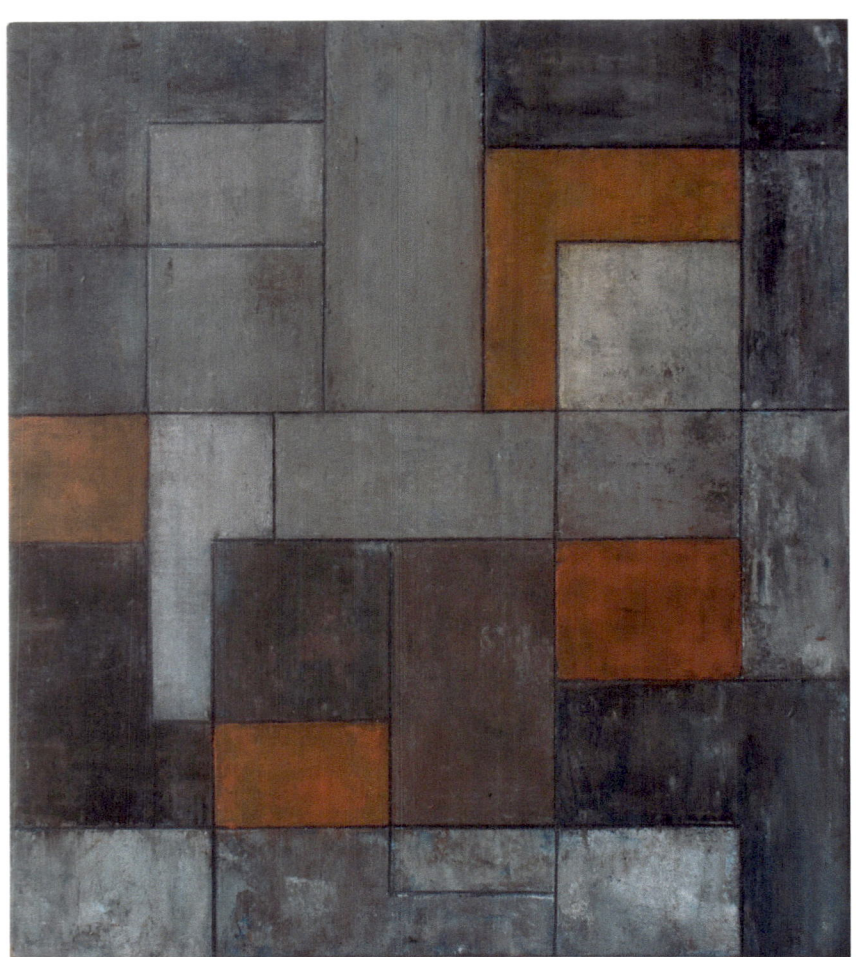

Stephen Cimini
patchouli 14 x 16 x 3 inches 2014
oil paint, cold wax medium on canvas

Candy LeSeur Sibver Streak, monotype, 2014

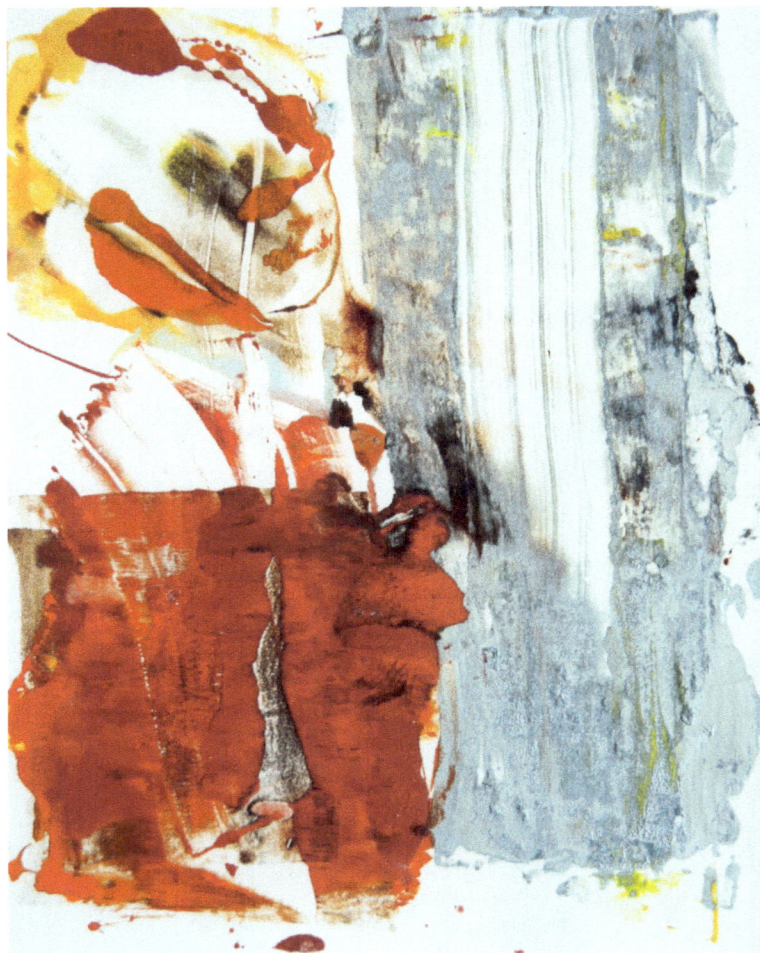

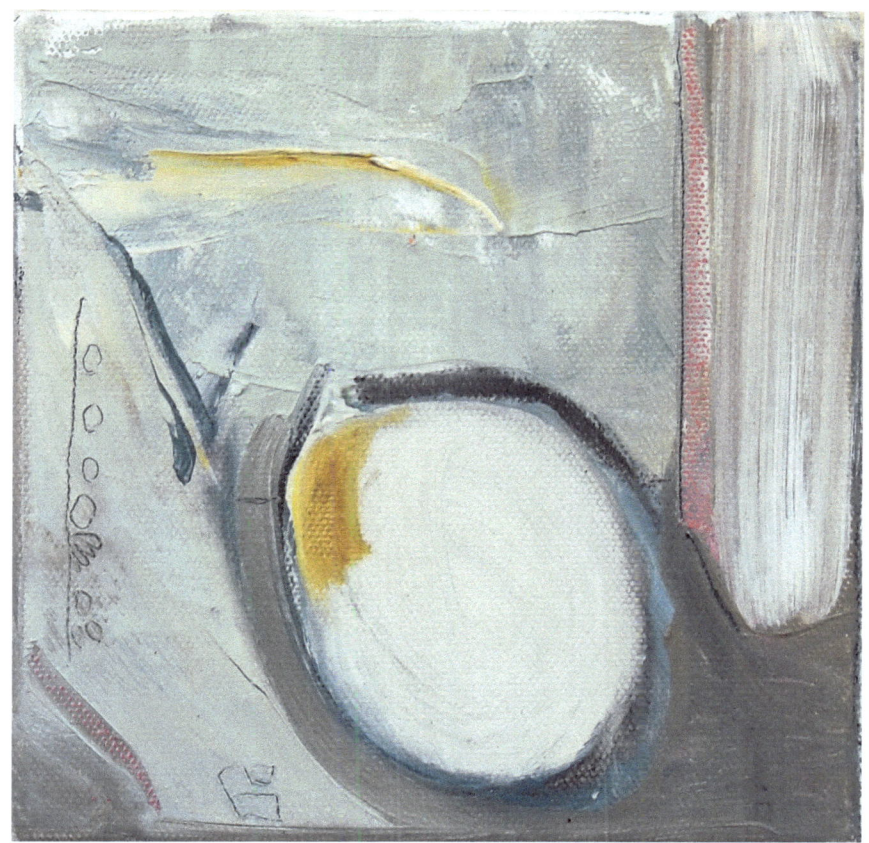

Gail Winbury, Chicken or Egg,, oil, 12x12, 2014.

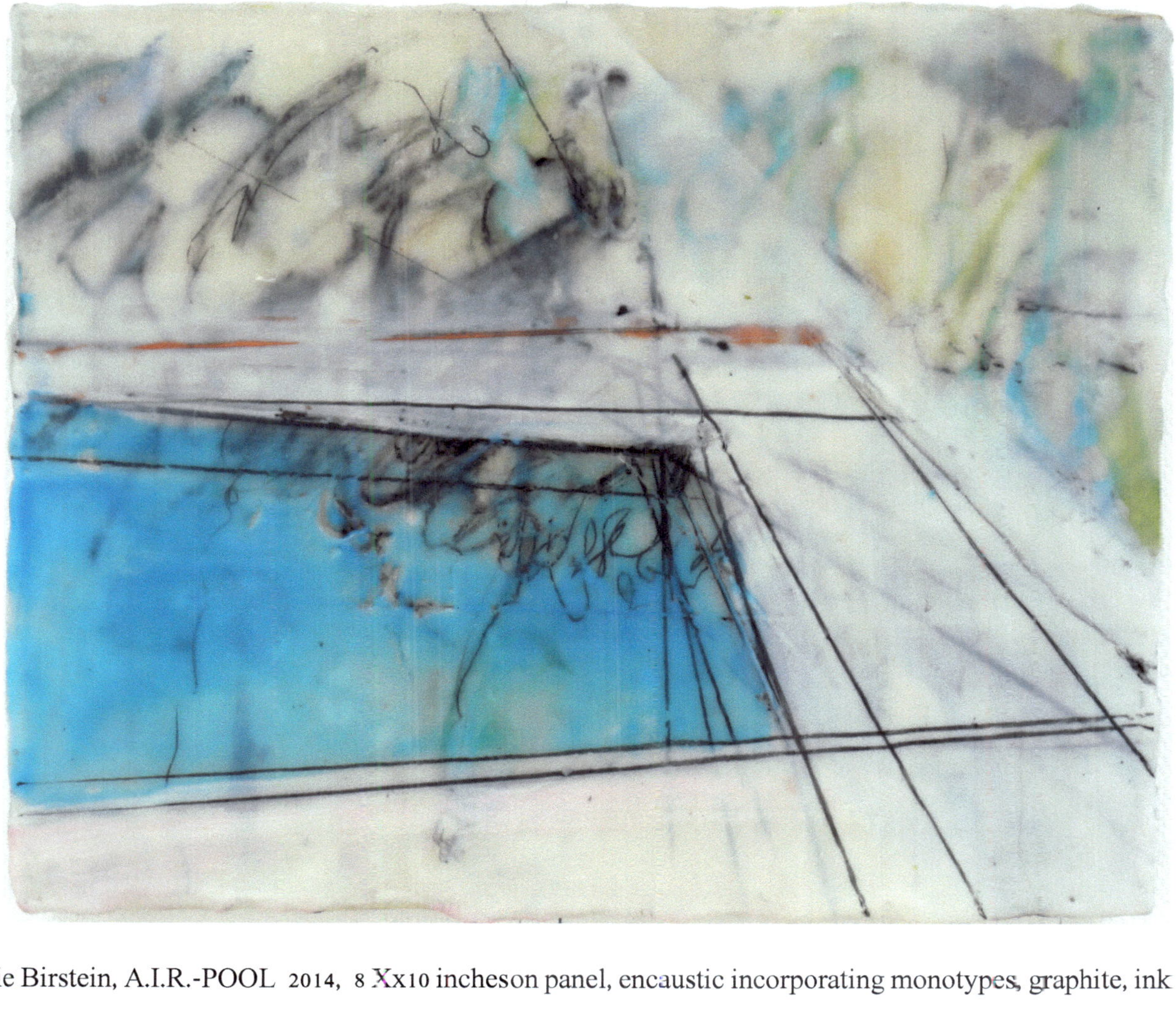

Binnie Birstein, A.I.R.-POOL 2014, 8 Xx10 incheson panel, encaustic incorporating monotypes, graphite, ink

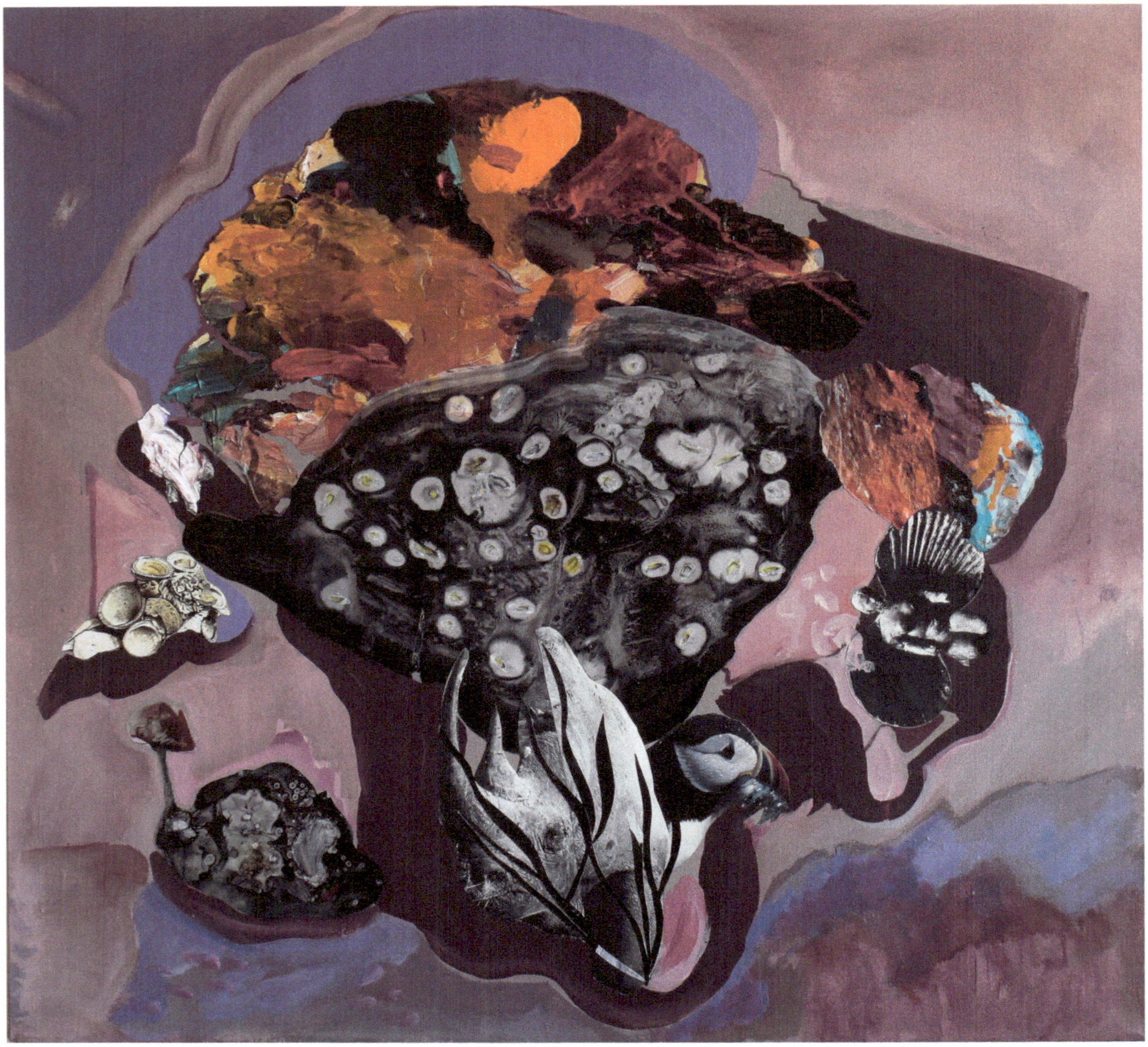

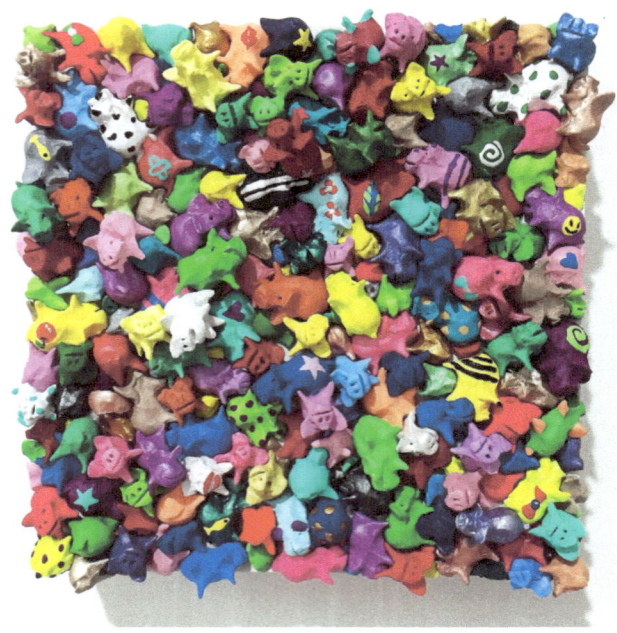

Jane Dell, Rhino, 28"x24", acrylic/collage on canvas,

Seunghwui Koo, Piggies, 2014, 6x6 inches

Gregory A. Stone - Full Moon Days - Acrylic - 16 x 20

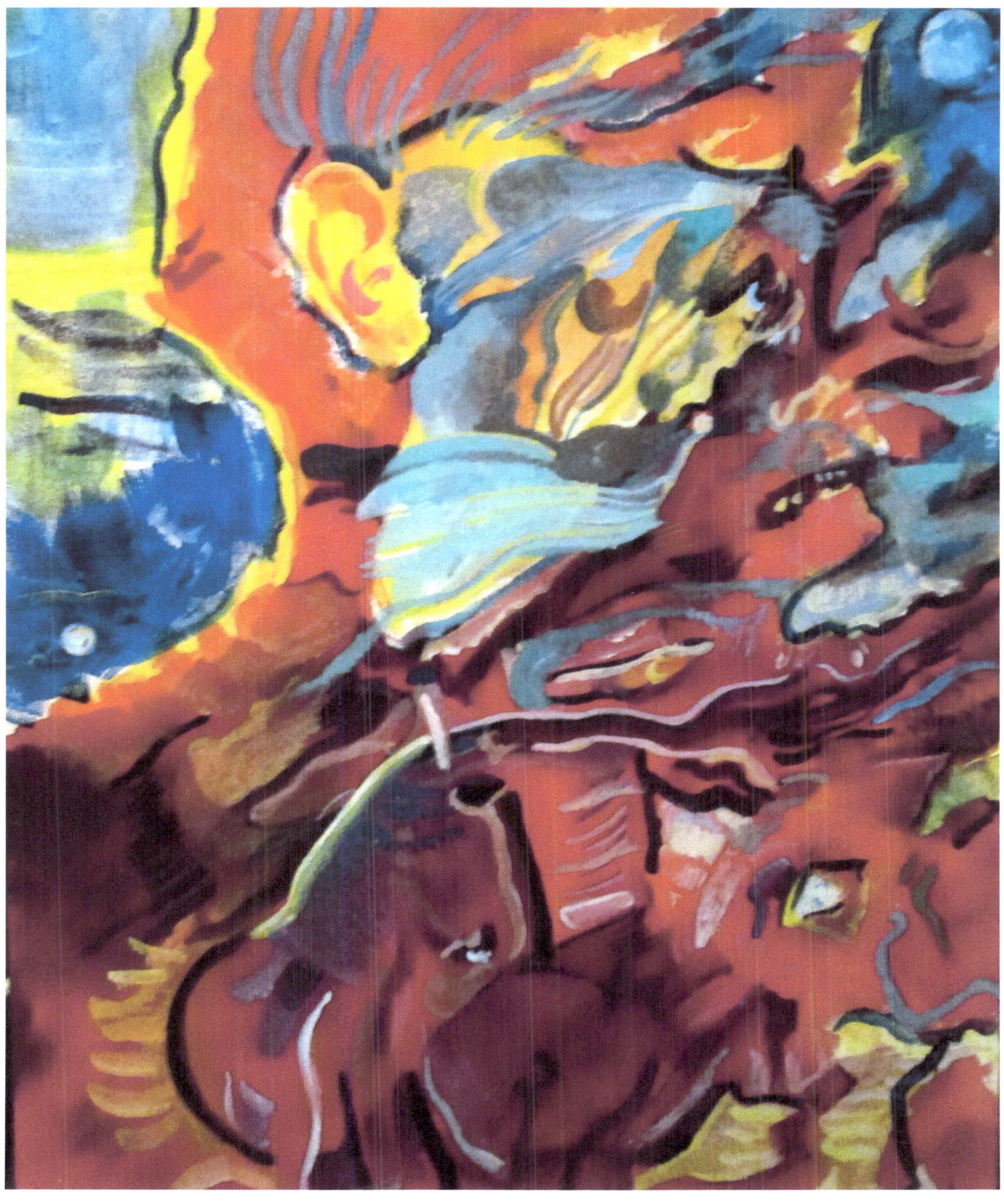

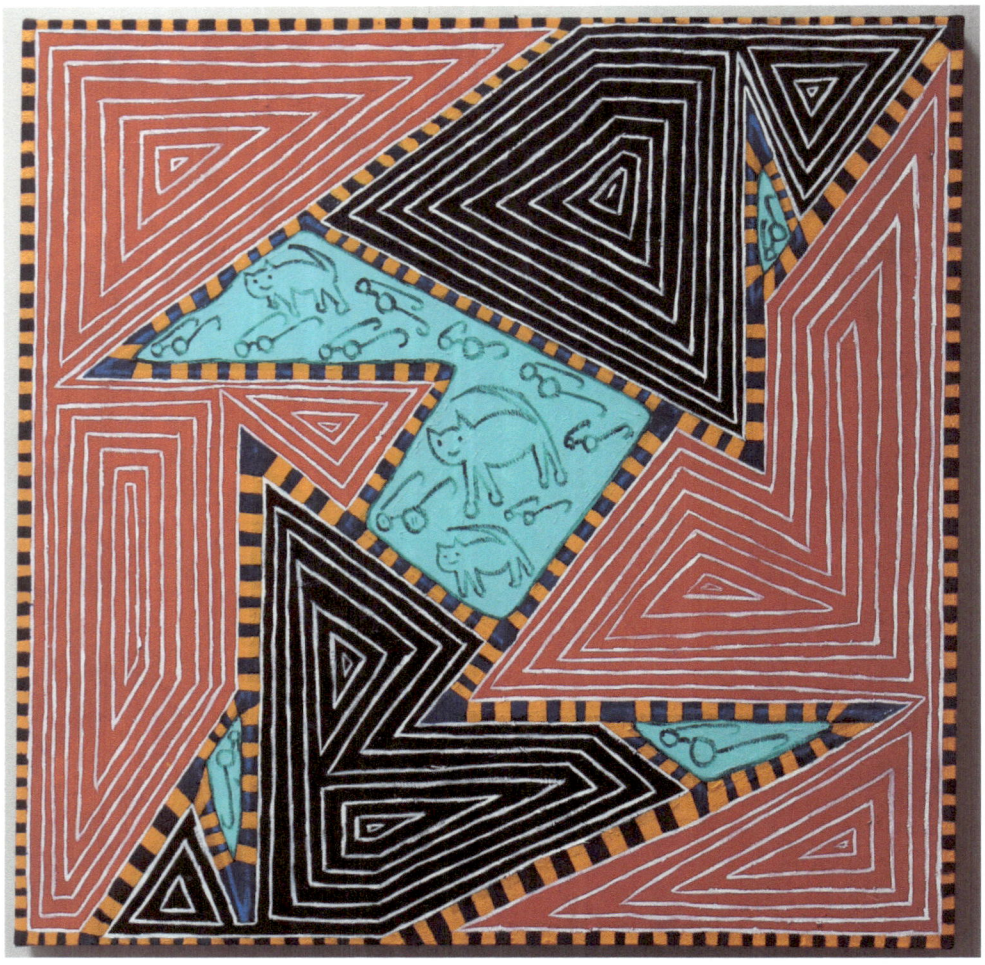

MegAtkinson-Picnic for Pliny 24 x 24 inches

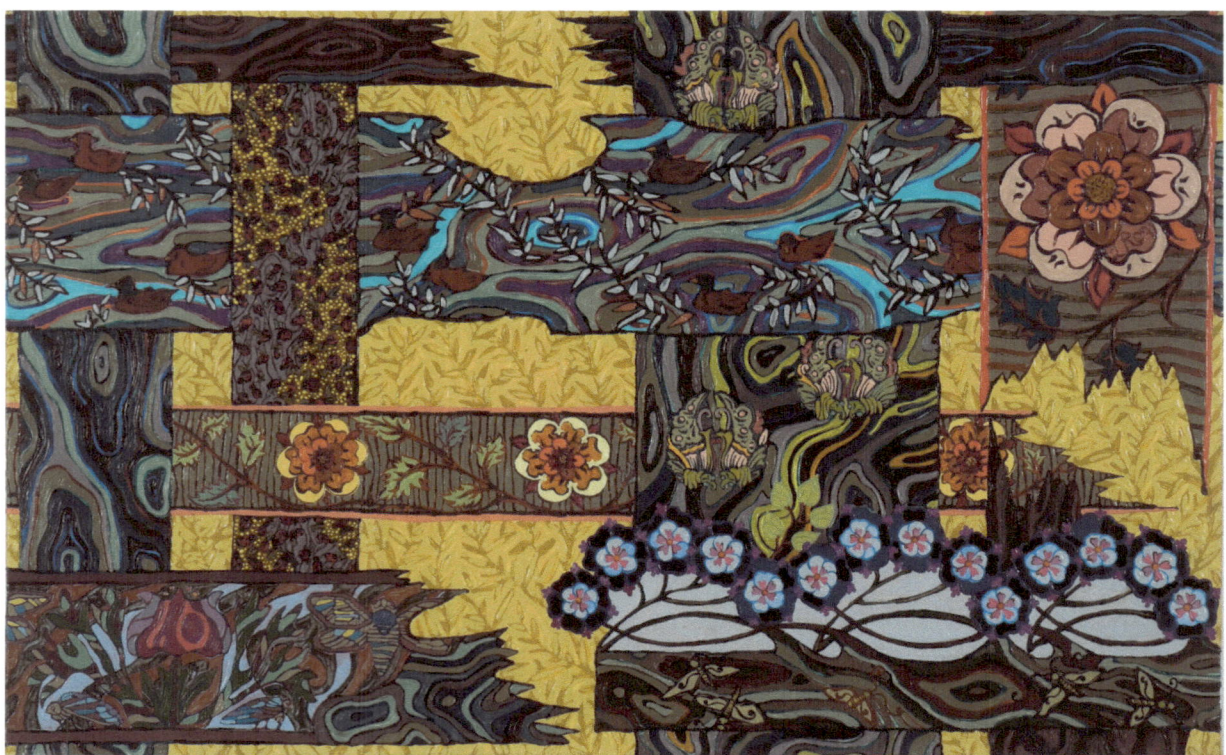

Laurie Riccadonna, Broken, oil on canvas, 18 x 24 inches

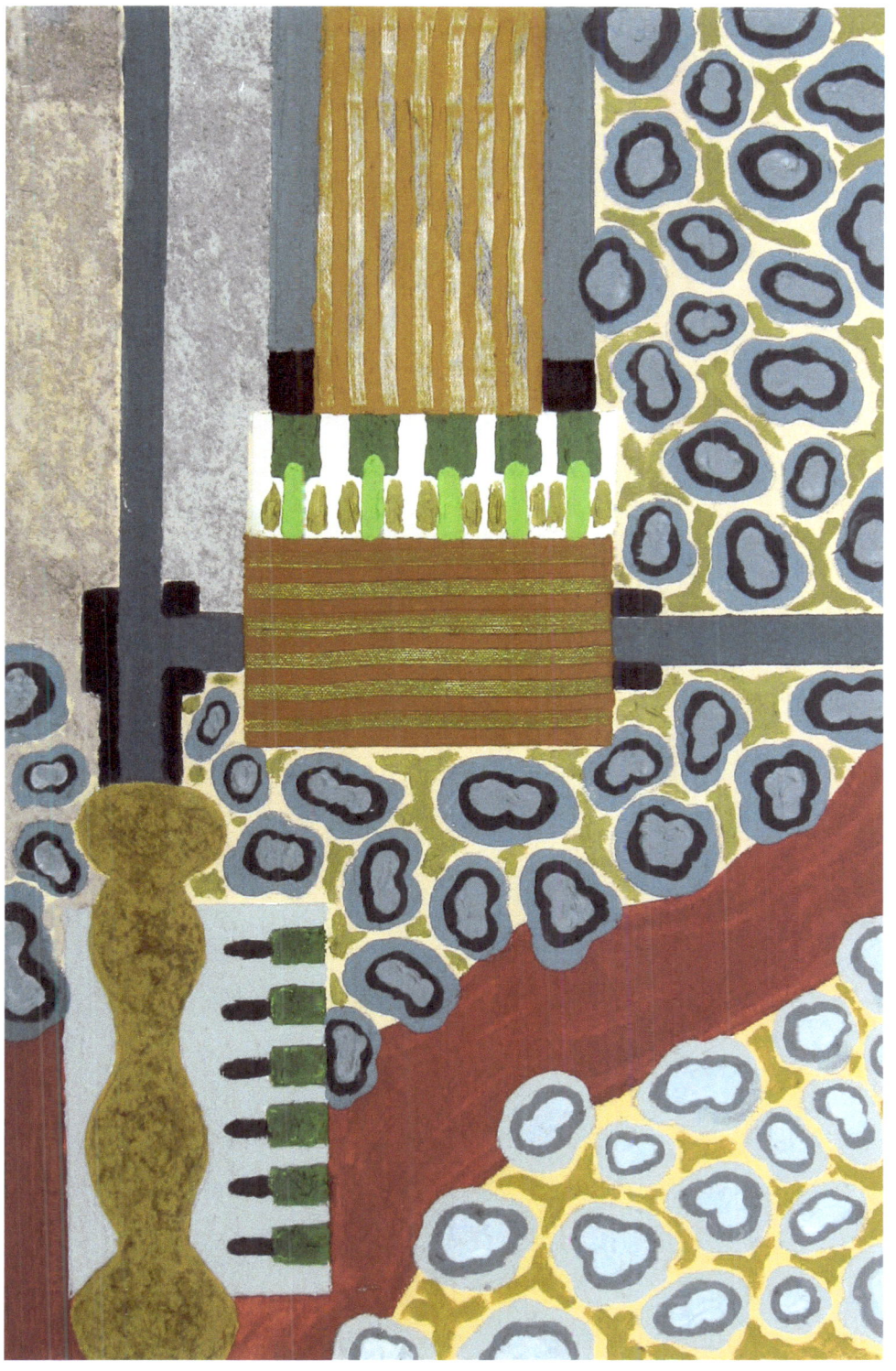

Len Merlo Fracking Rig On a River Bed 14"x22" Acrylic,collage,sand, on canvas

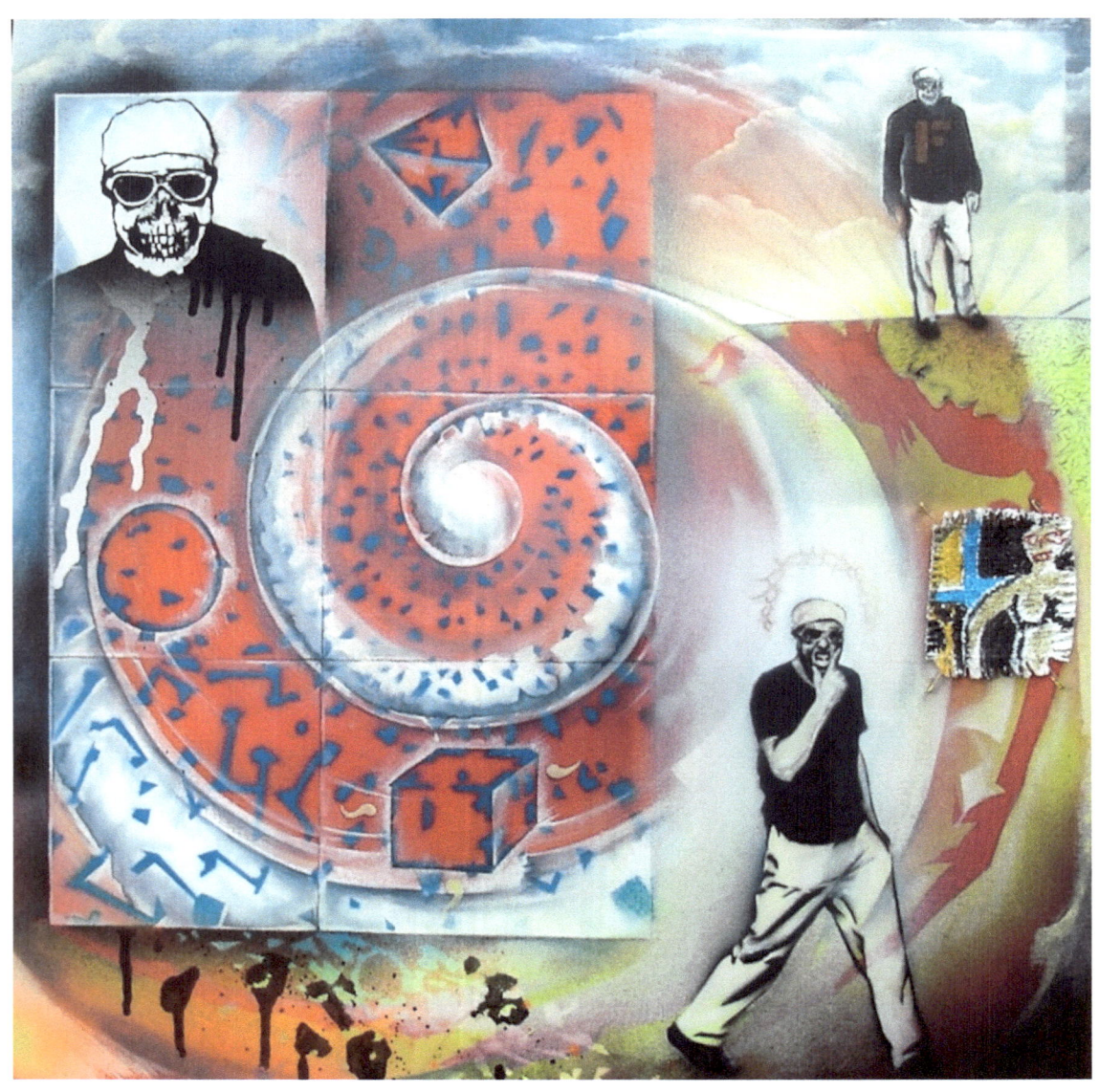

Dancing with Mr. ″D″Size: 20″ x 20″ Mixed Media on canvas

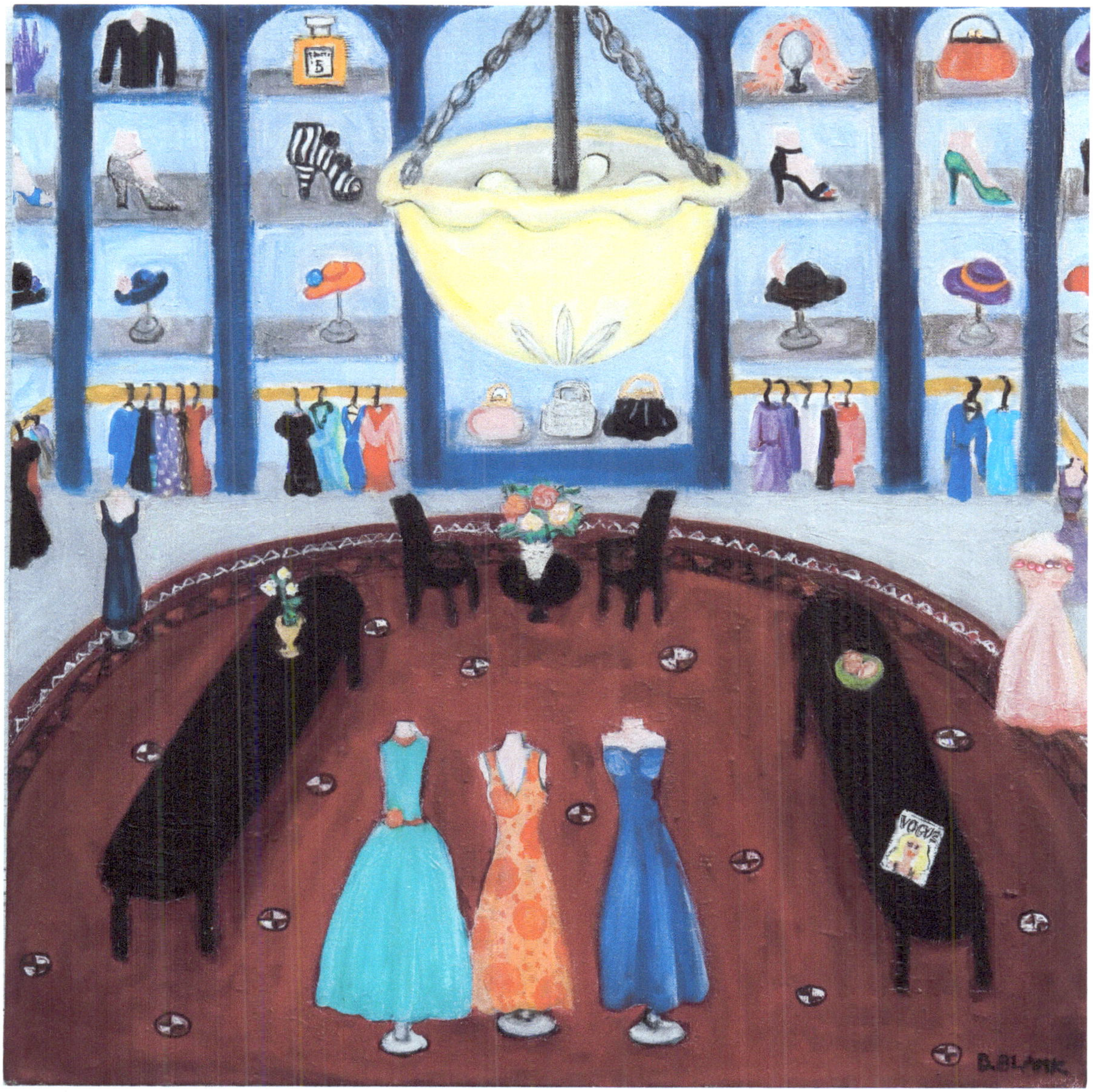

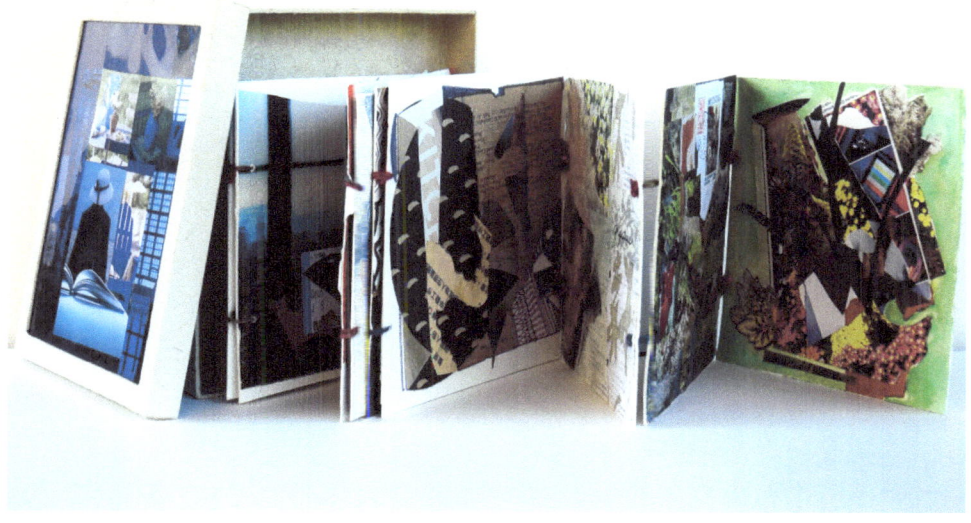

Bette Blank.Gown Salon.2014. 24 X 24, oil

Alice Harrison, BookinaBox 1

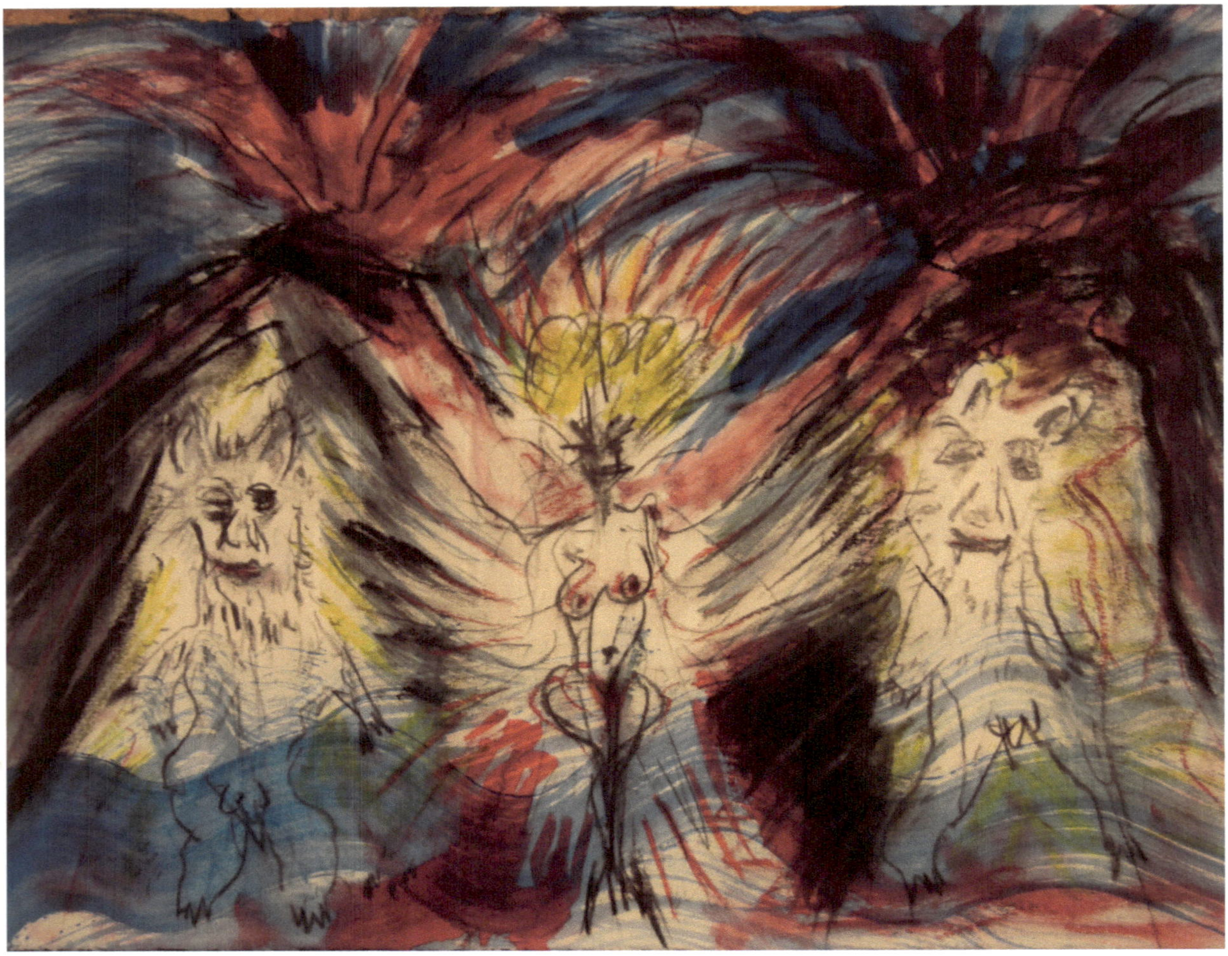

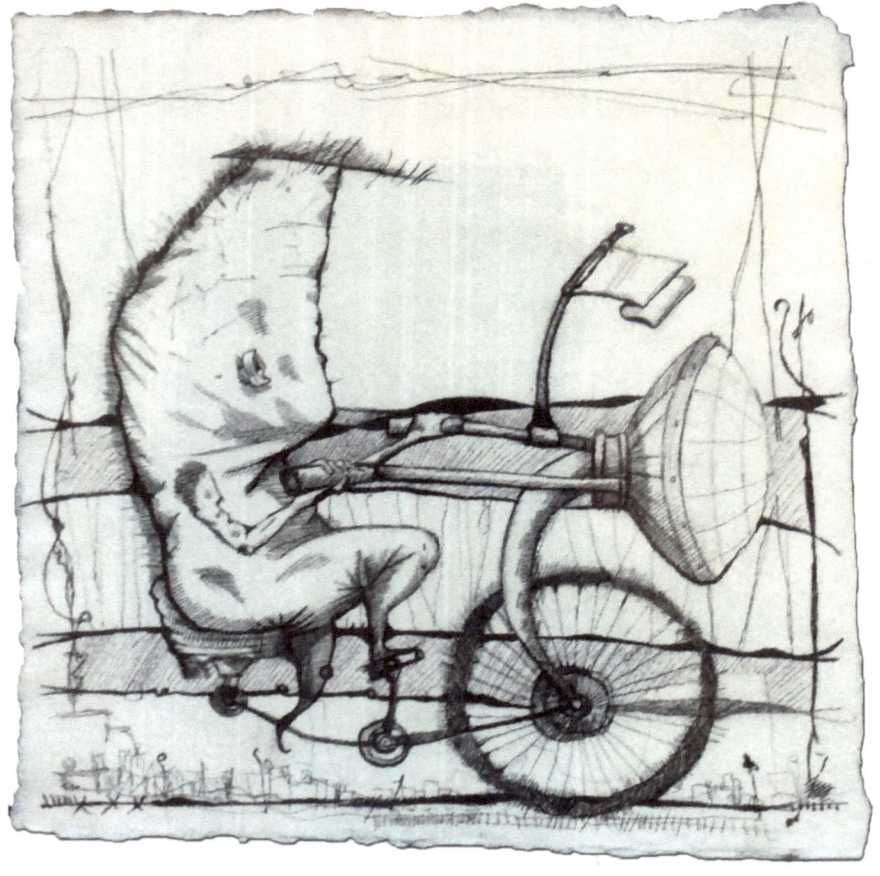

Buck Henri Dancing Bears and Pele the fire Godess at Holuhraun Eruption ~ Iceland 2014

Cheryl Gross, Randolph, ink on paper 2014

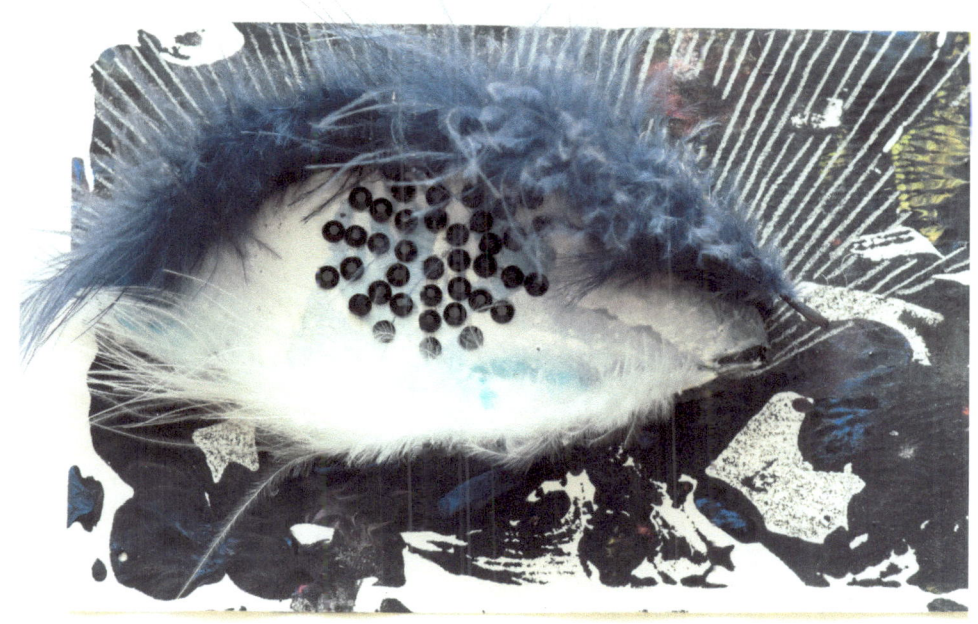

Margaret Weber EAF 7961, 2014

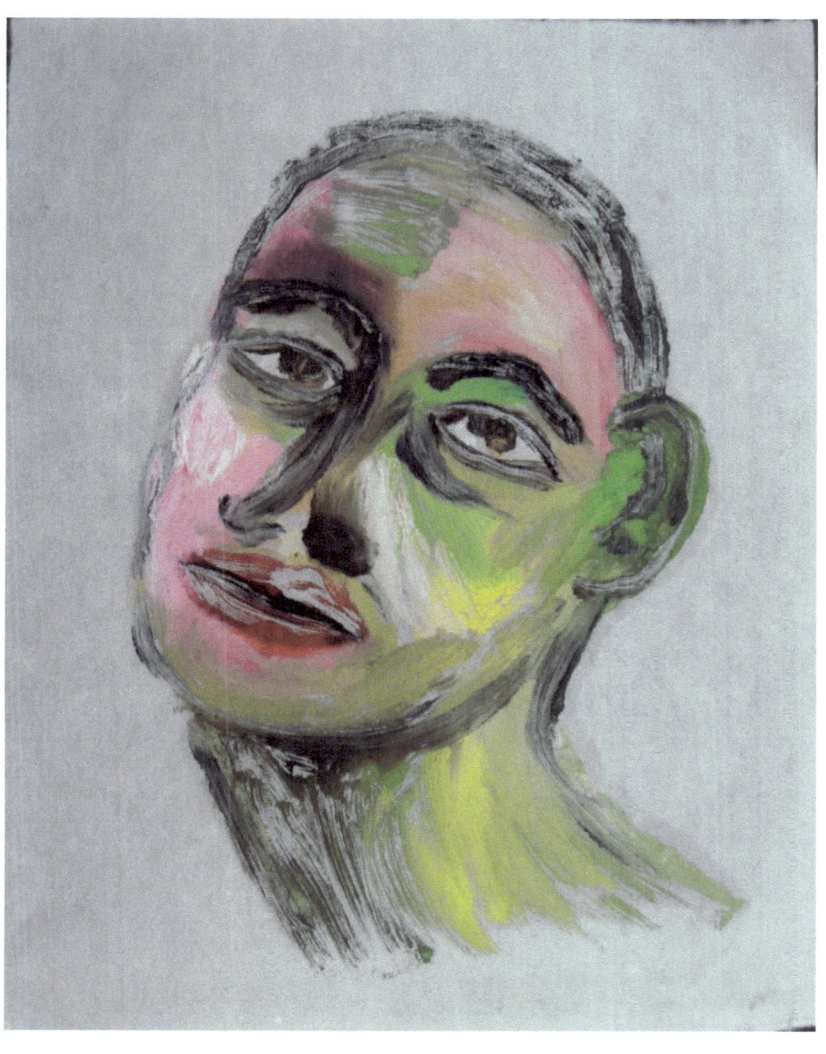

Theresa DeSalvio, Monoprint 6414 I, 9x12 unframed, oil paint on Japanese paper,

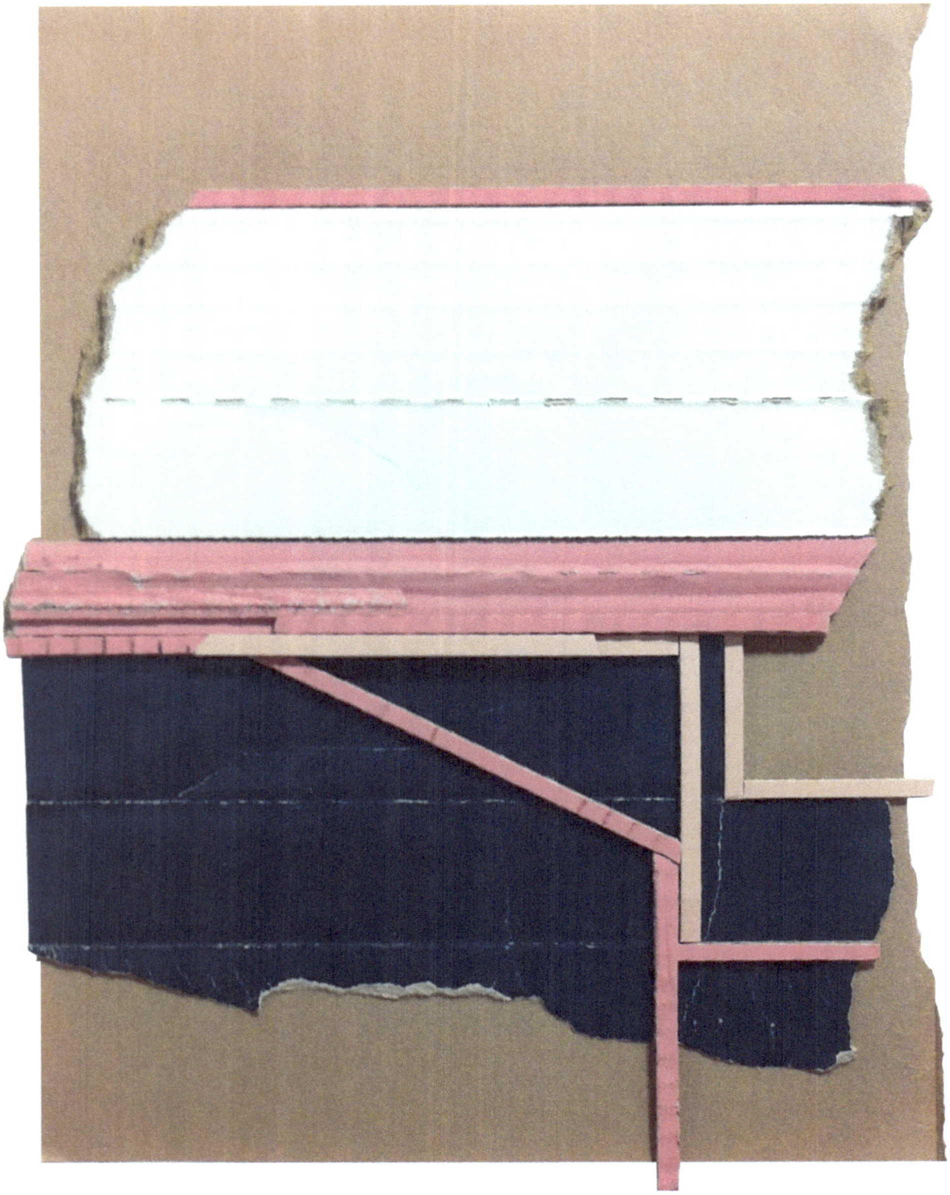

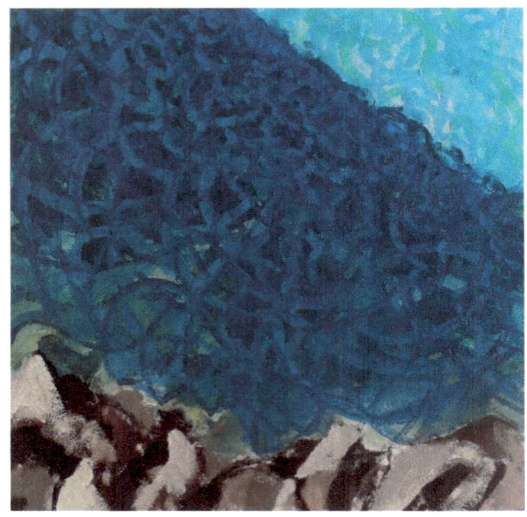

RyanSarahMurphy-shift-2014-11 x 8 inches

Elliot MarkellOn Shore #2, 2013, oil on panel, 12″x12 inches

Eileen Ferara
Cape May Point-whelk casings
6in x 6in
mixed media (oil, drawing, collage)

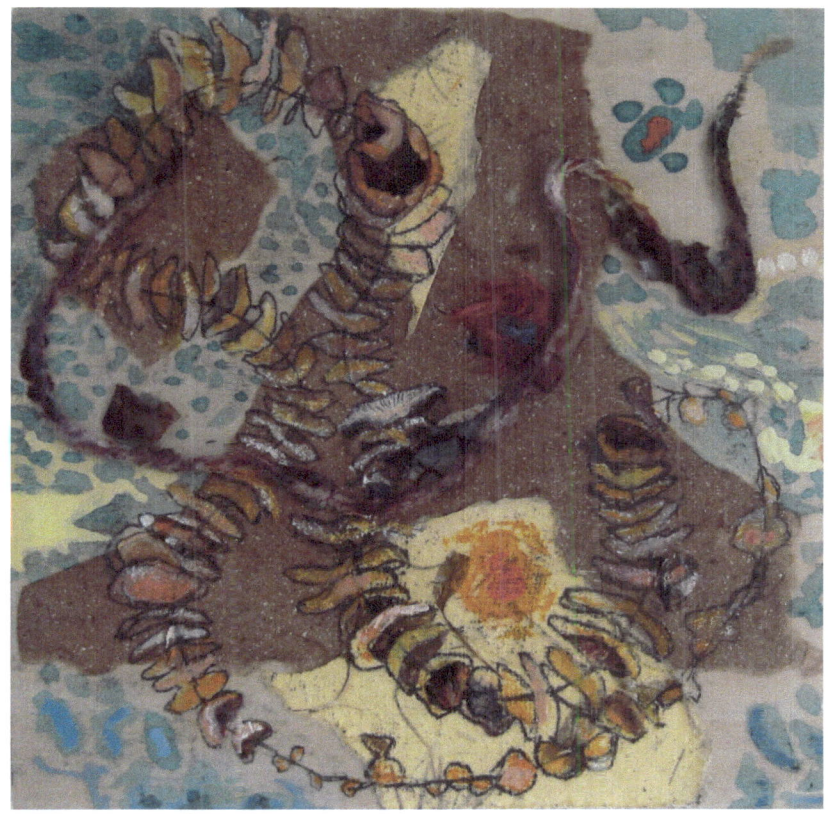

Steve Singer Clubbed Cherry
watercolors   24″ X 18 inches

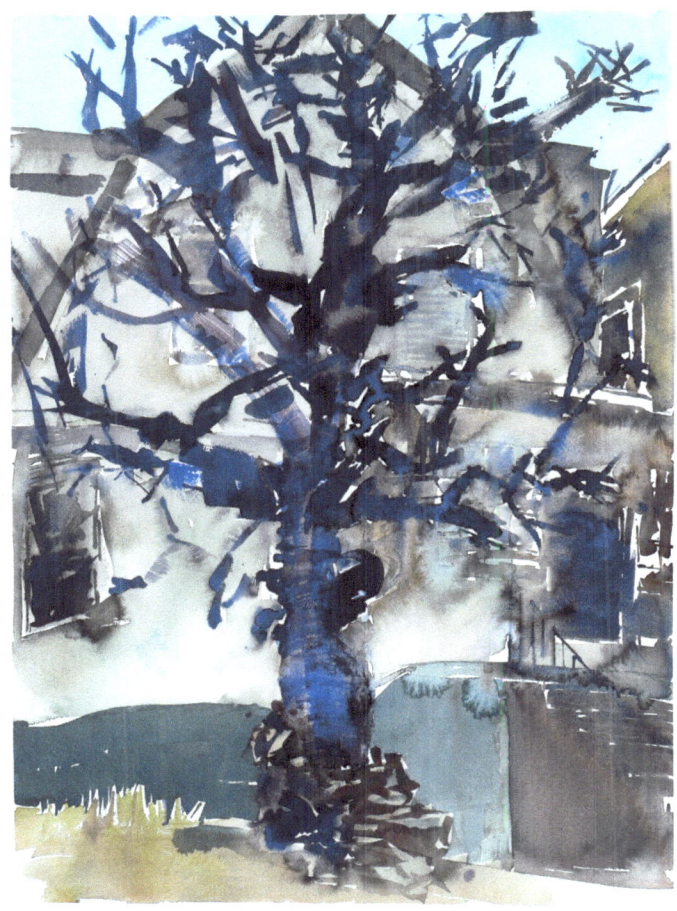

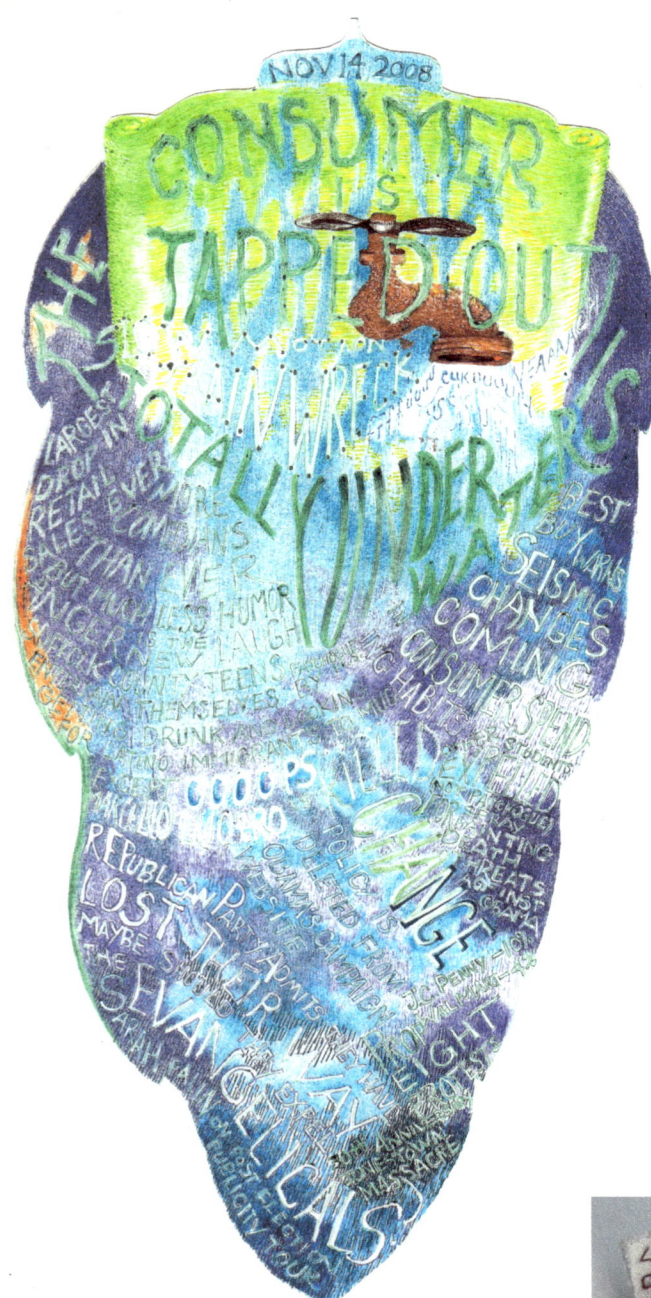

Barbara Stork,
 No 35b Consumer is Tapped Out,
Inks on paper, 9 x 4 inches 2014

Pat Dahlman Patricia Love 2011 17 x 17 inches

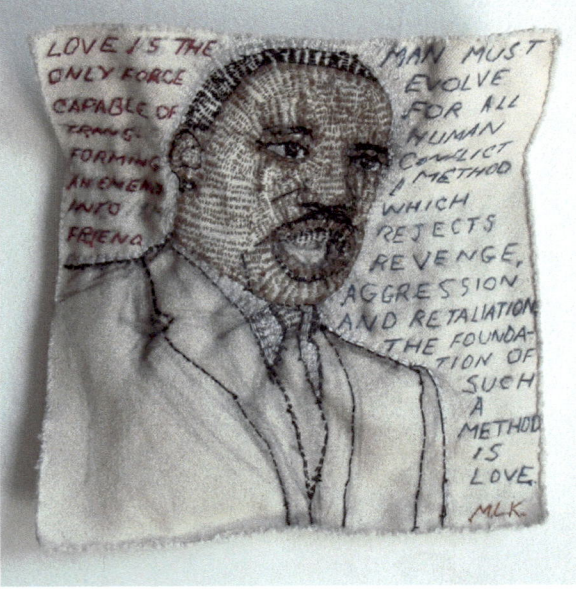

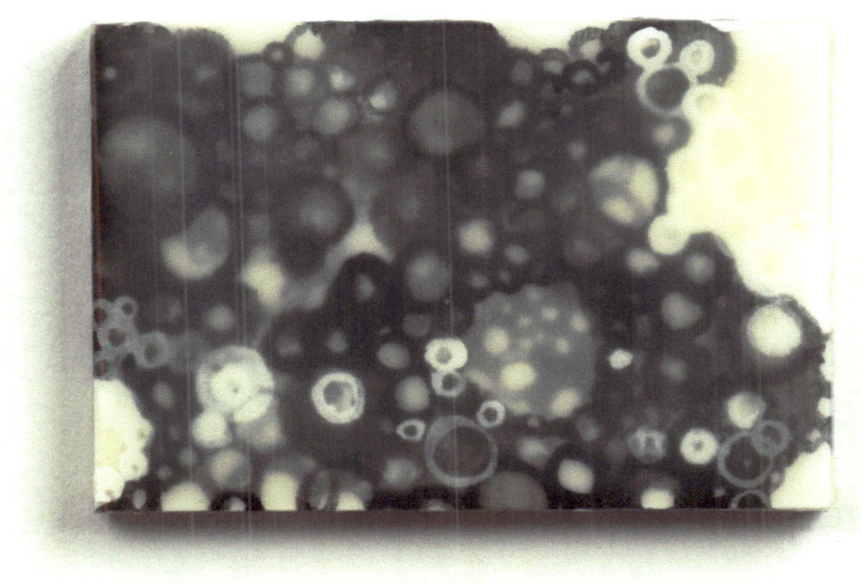

Beth Dary Teem Egg Tempera and beeswax on panel 11" x 11" (artwork is 2" x 3") 2013

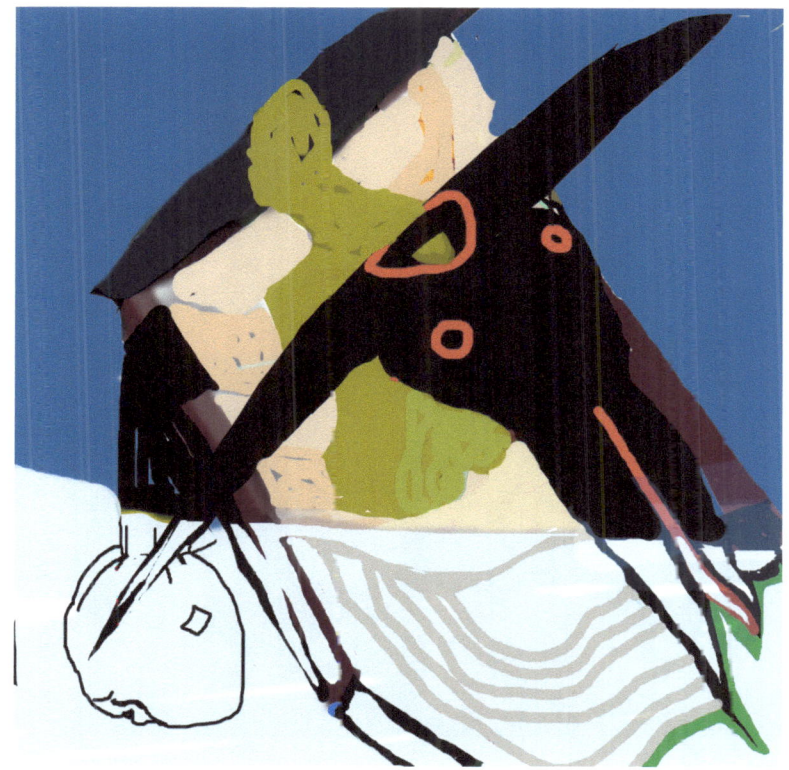

Carol Radsprecher Big Mouth 2014 12x12

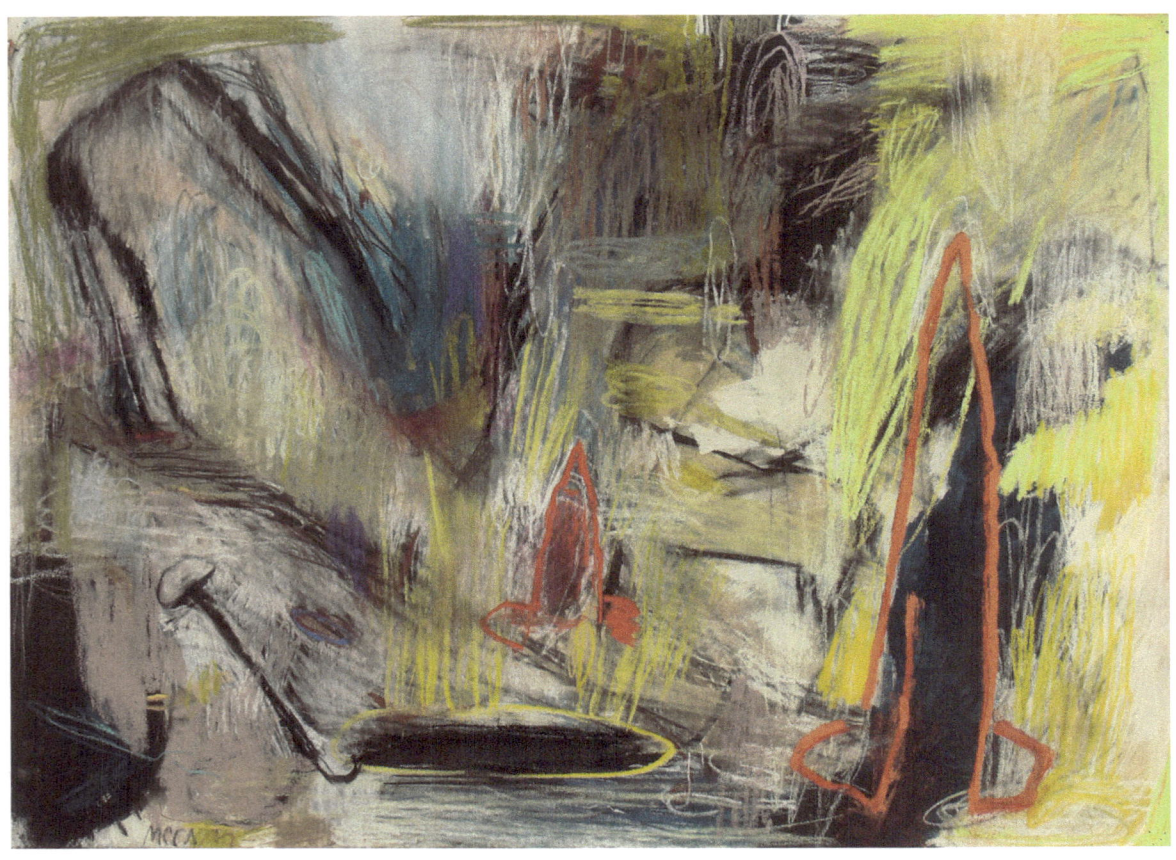

LadyMcCrady   Inventory Hole 072 2014 20 x 27 inches pastel on paper

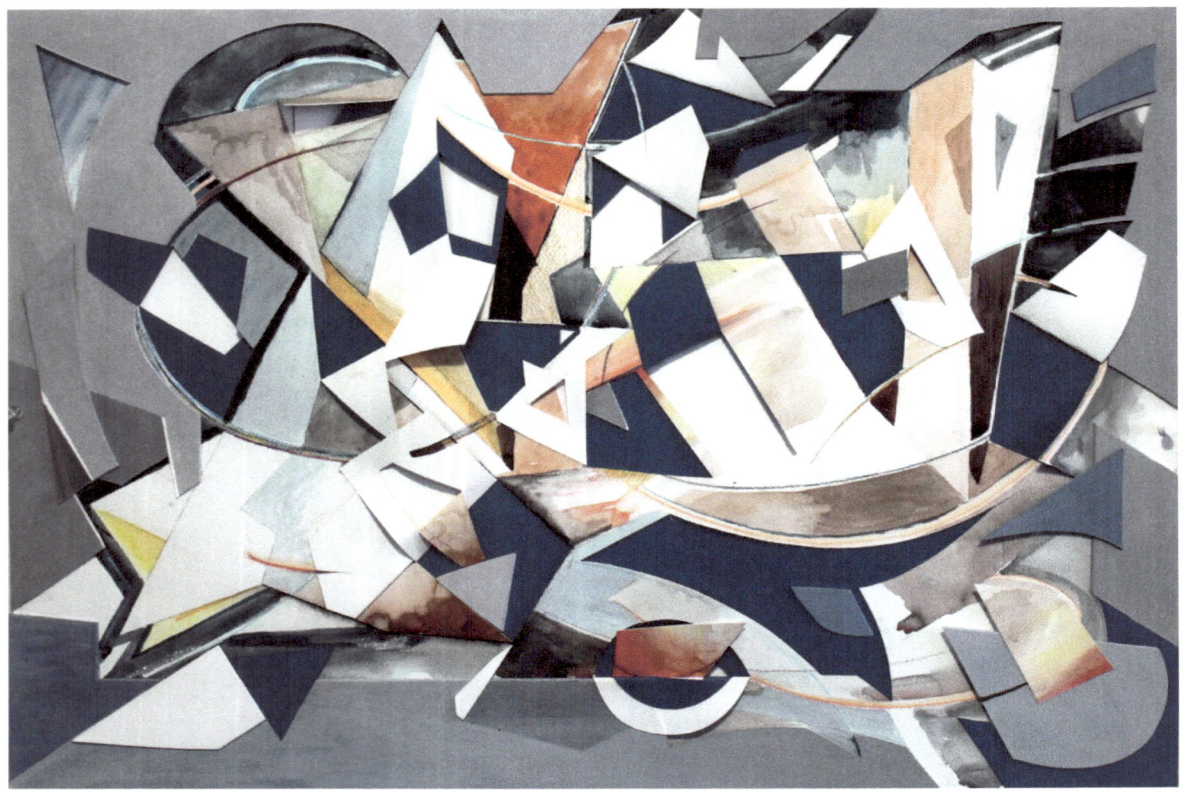

Gianluca Bianchino optic space 2, collage

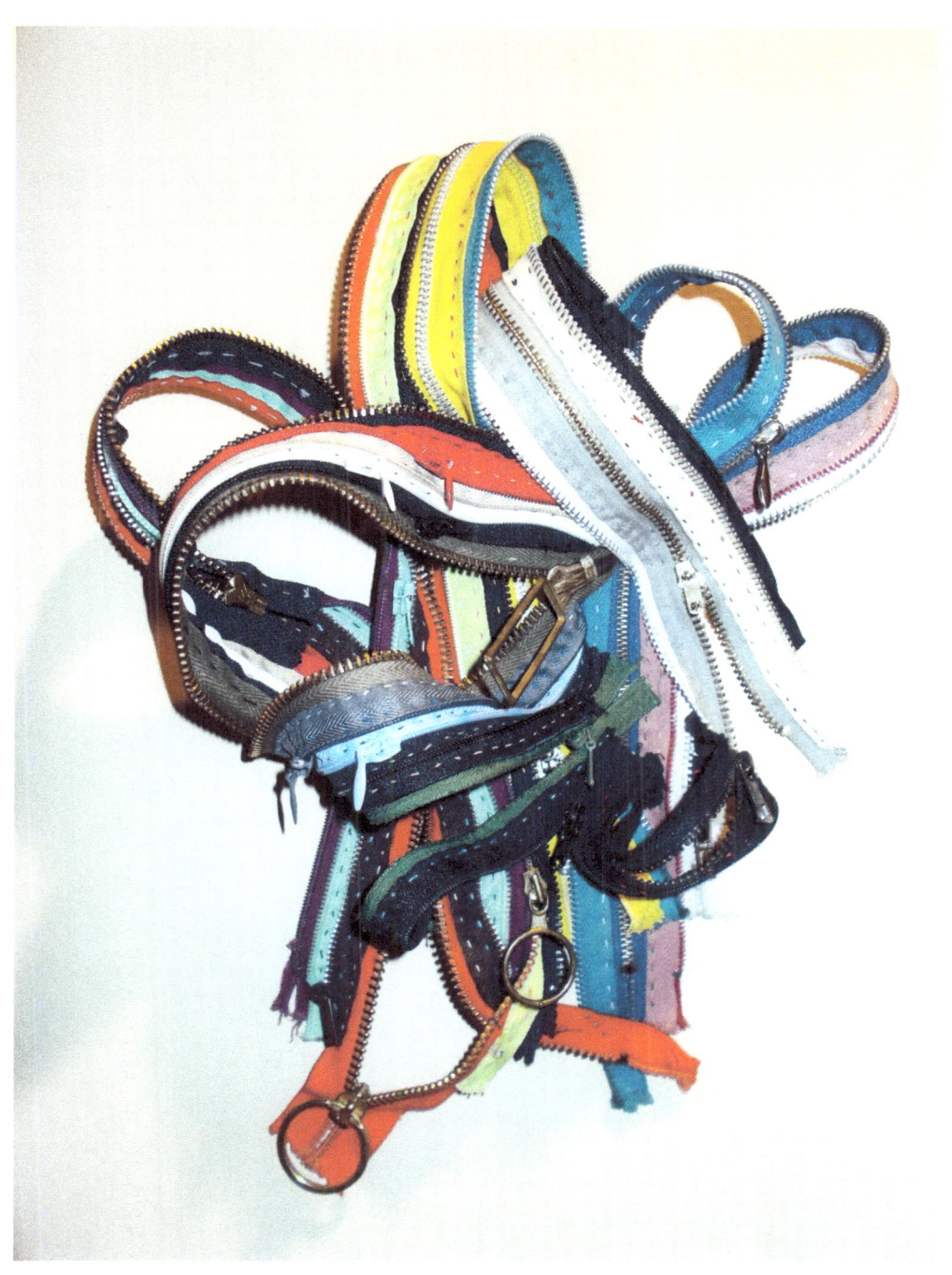

Julie Mchargue, Fly, materials-zippers, 2014, 14 x 8 x 2.5 inches

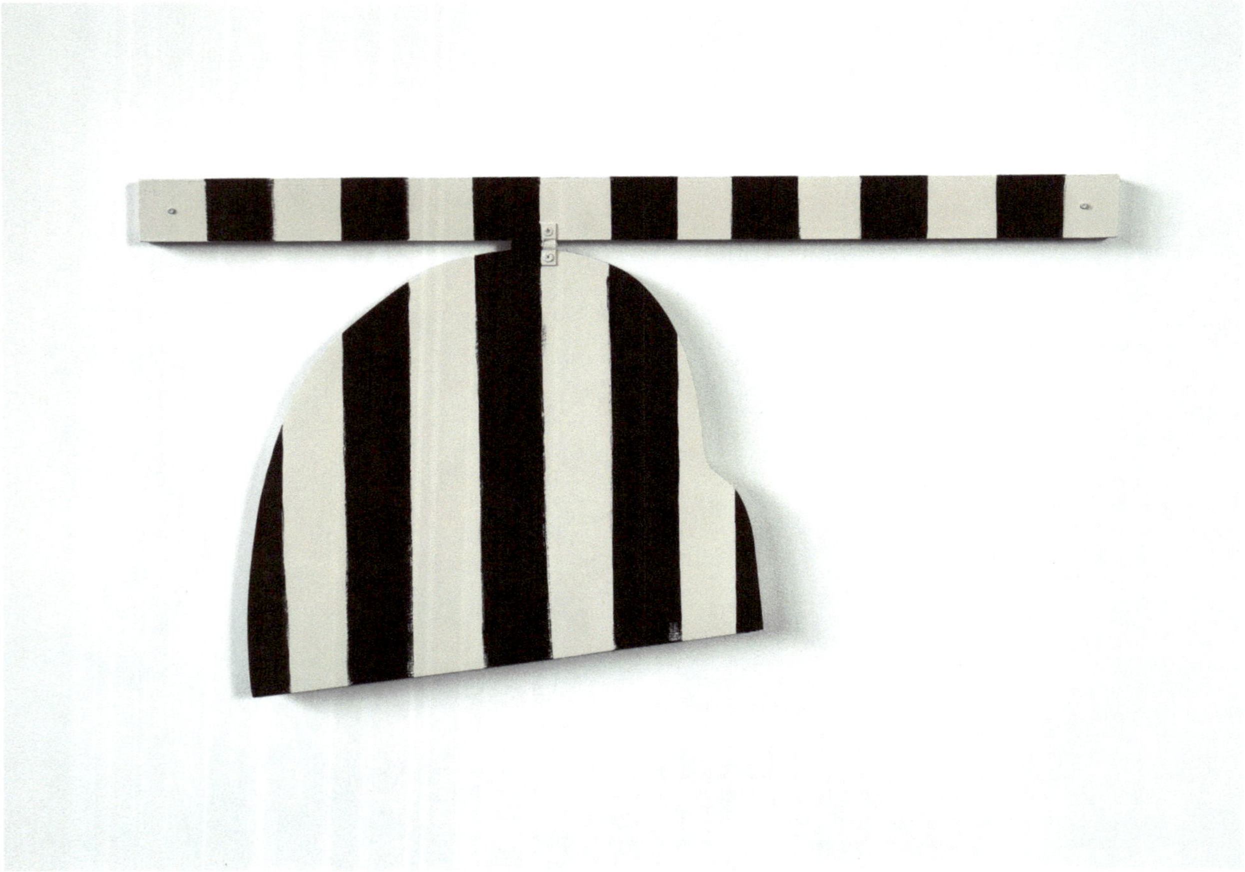

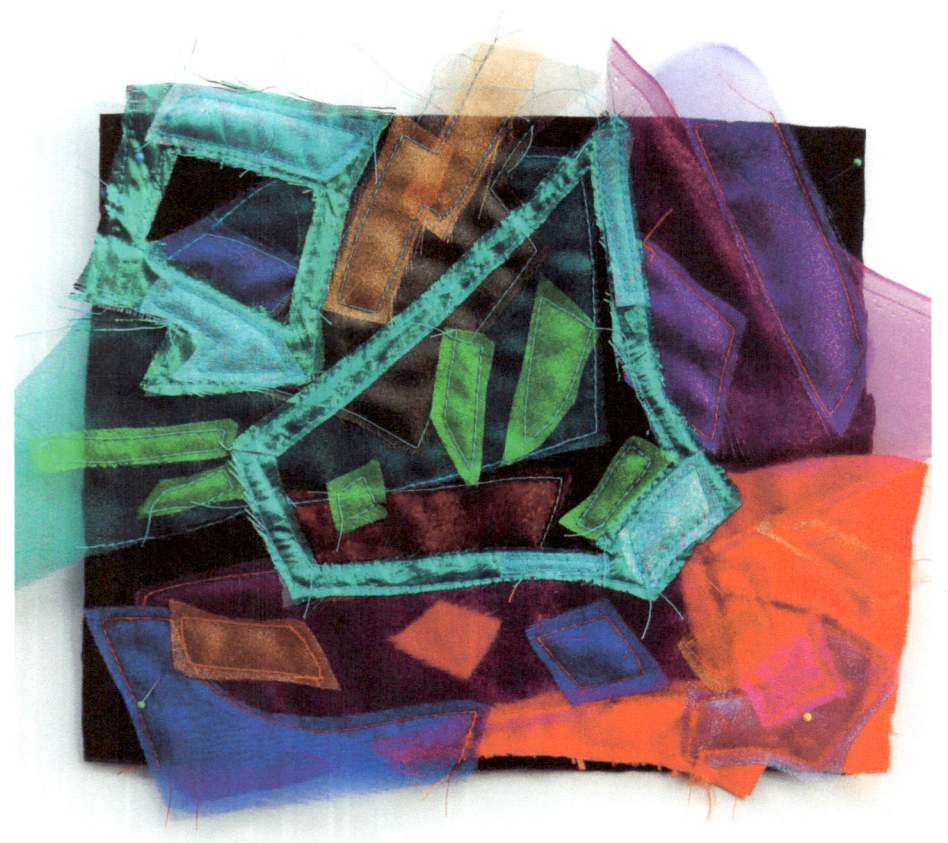

ChristinaTenaglia untitled 2013 23 x 1 x 11 inches

Mollie Thonneson "V of I" 2013   13" x 13" Framed

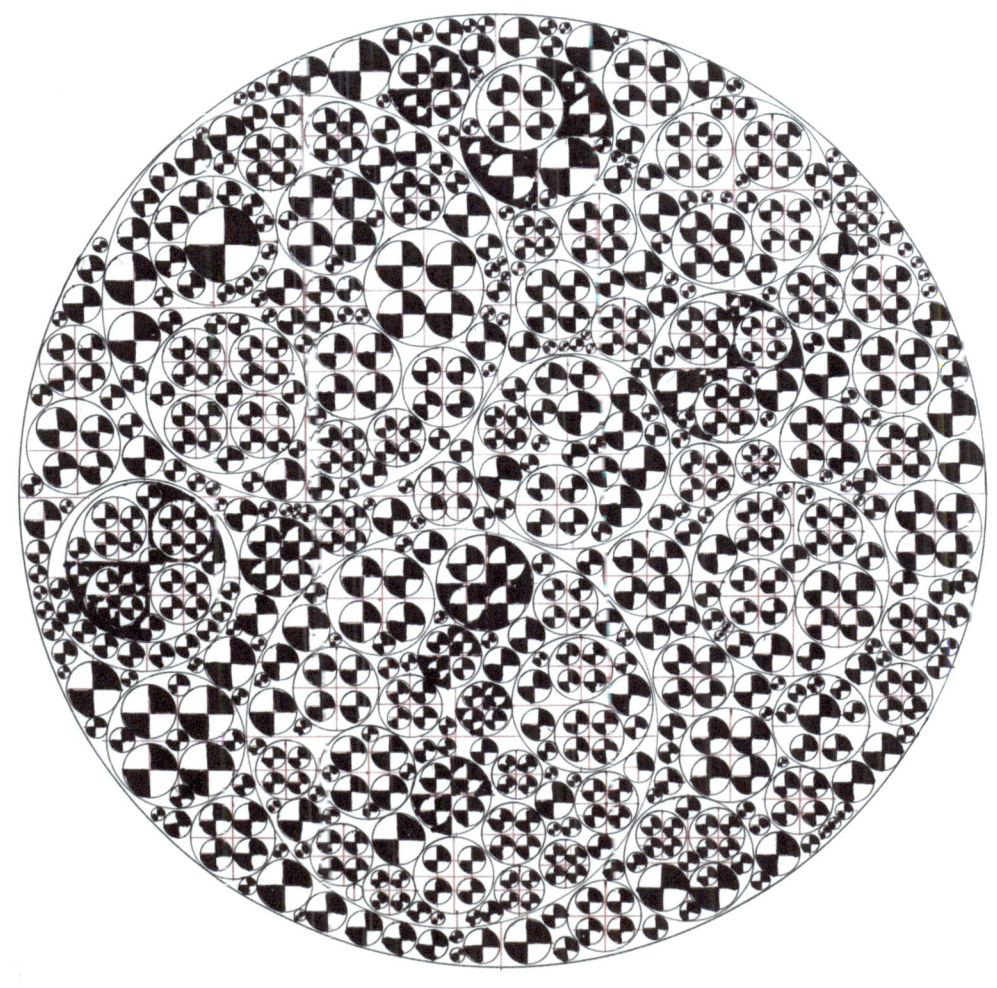

Tim Main FIRST SPIN 11 x 14 inches Ballpoint and Sharpie 2014

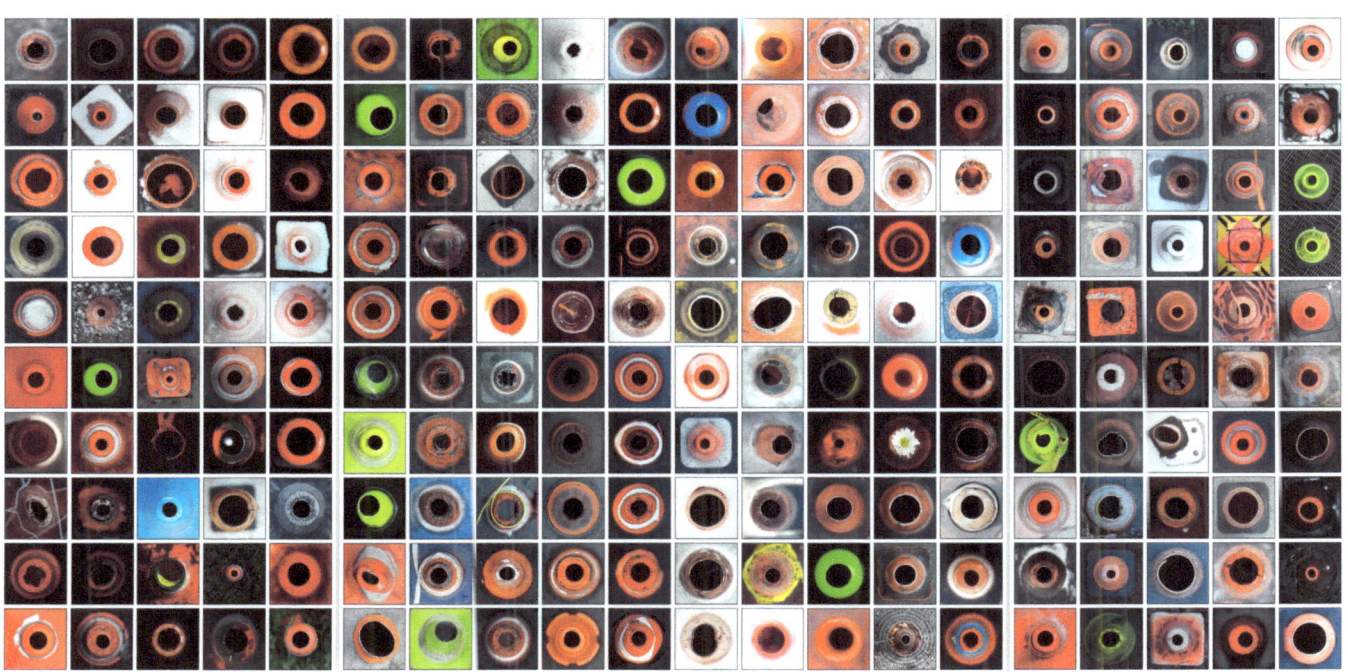

PeterEmerick, Unititled (2008-11, Top50), colorprint, 2012, 24 x 12 inches

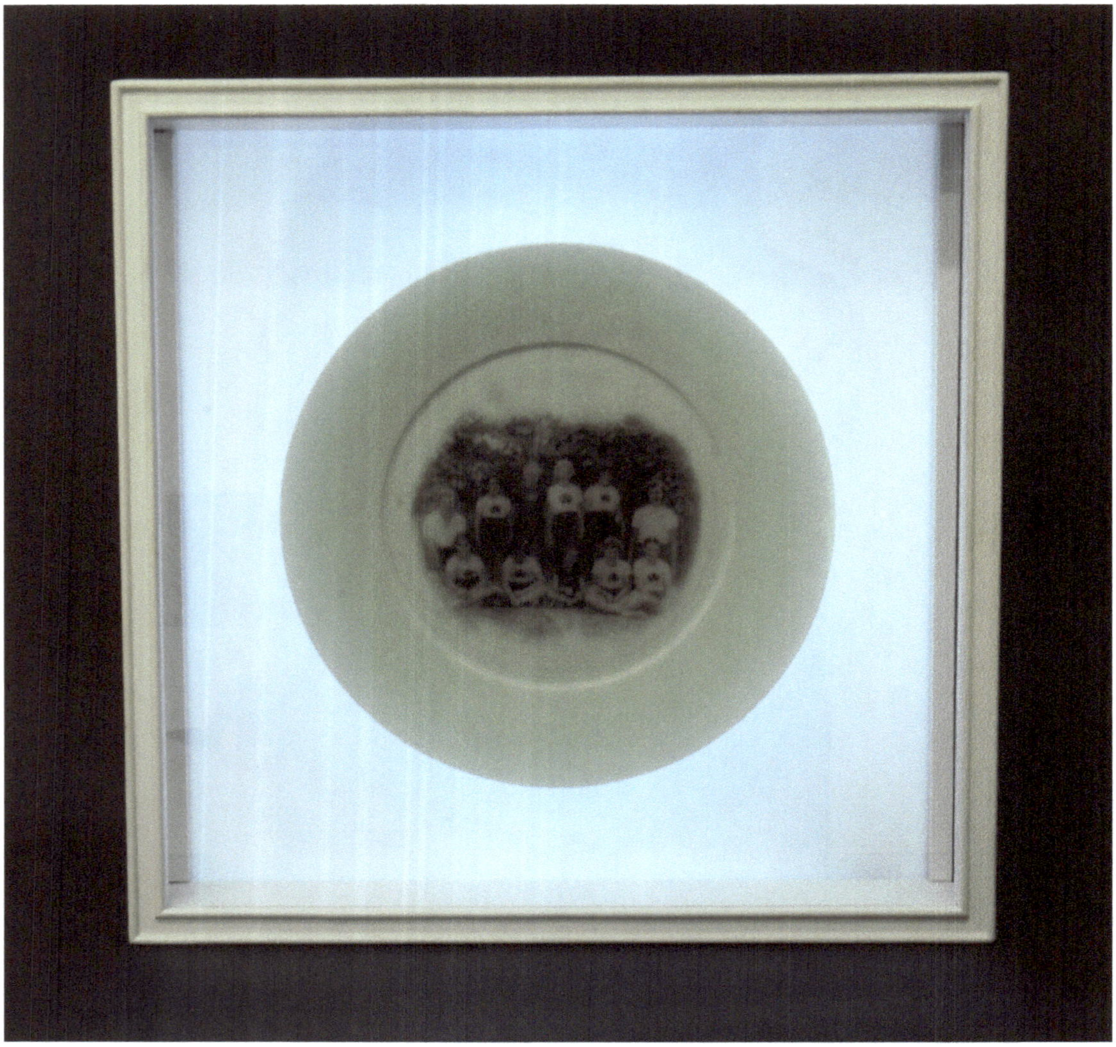

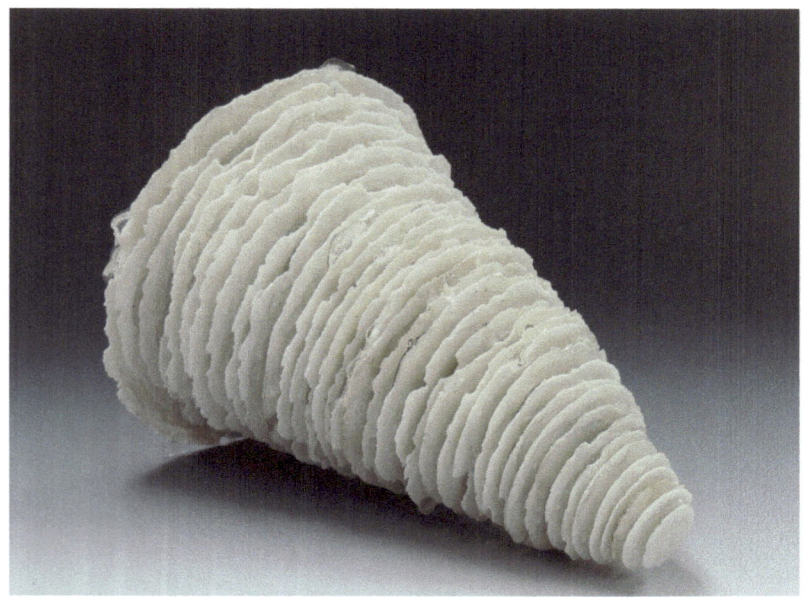

Jeremy Coleman Smith , Collectible (Nostalgic) 2013 Ink on polystyrene plate wood, led lights glass 18 x 18 inches

ChrisVivas Untitled 2014   5 x 4 x 7 inches

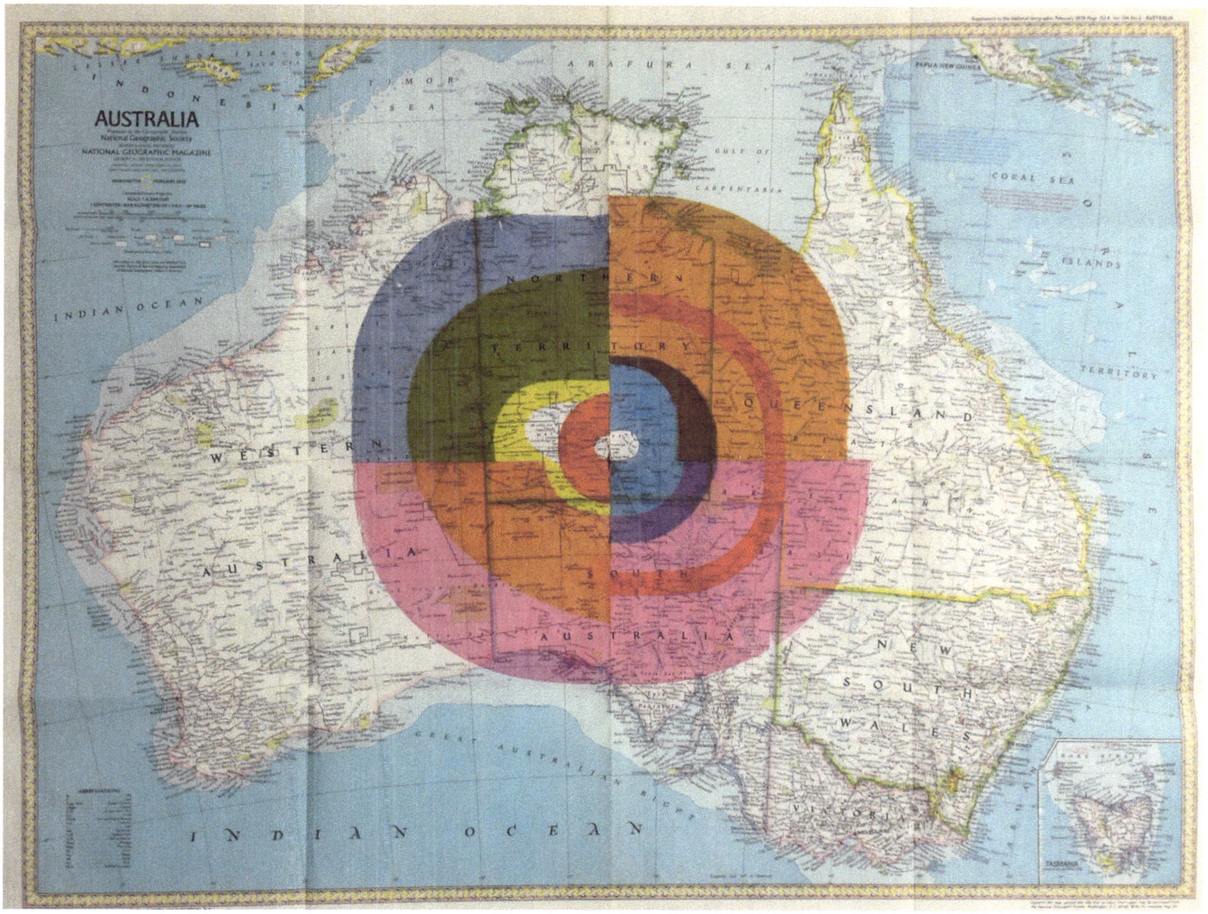

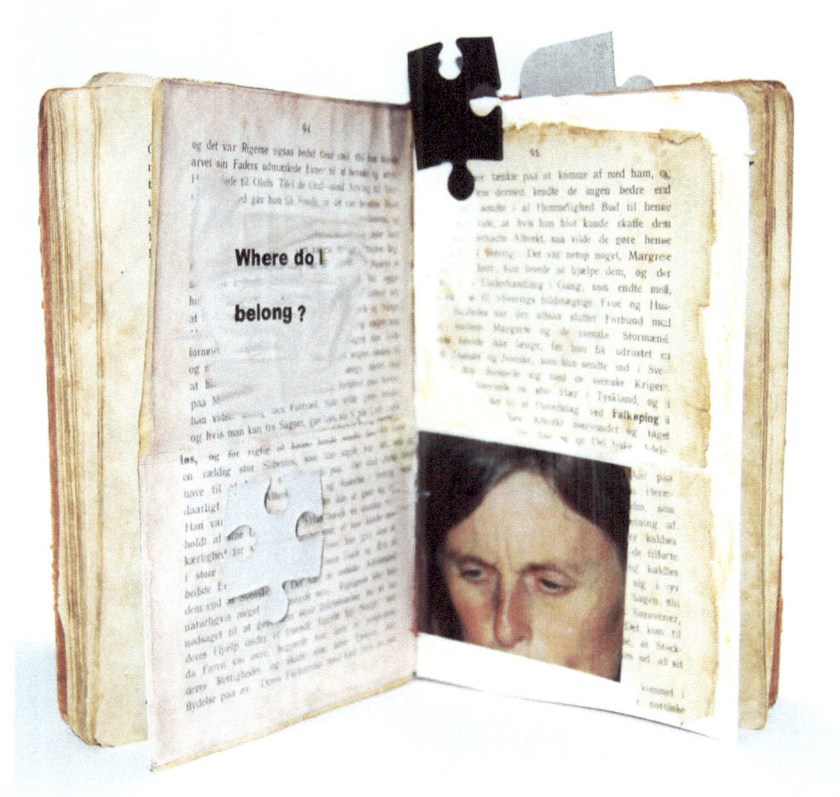

Sam Larson, Map-Australia 2014 29 x 22 inches

Aileen Bassis, Danish Story, book

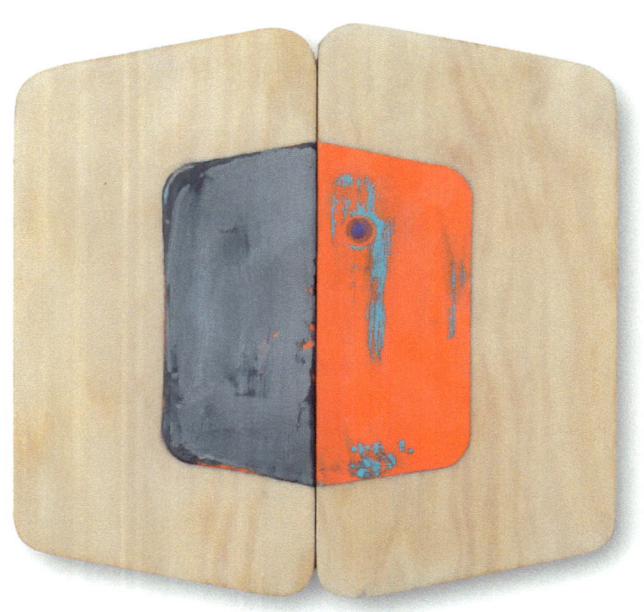

Ruth Hiller, Perspective on 1.0.1.5 2014 12 x 12 inches. Wood panels

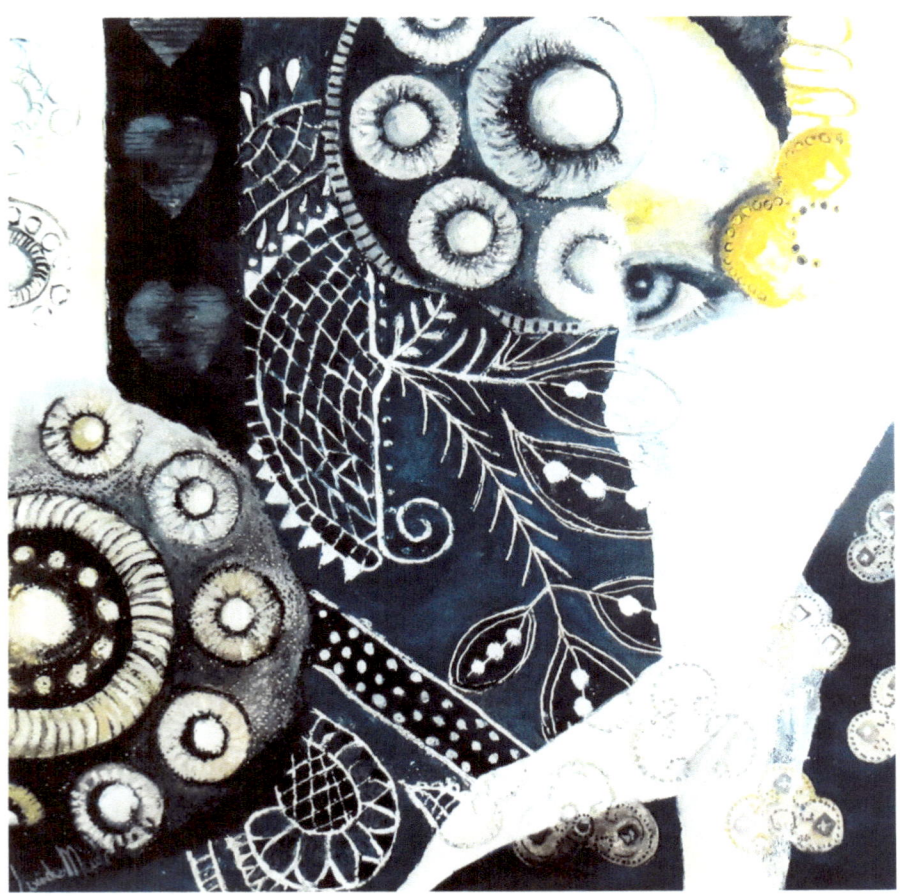

Loura van der Meule,   Zeeuwse boerenknoop , 1 mixed media on board

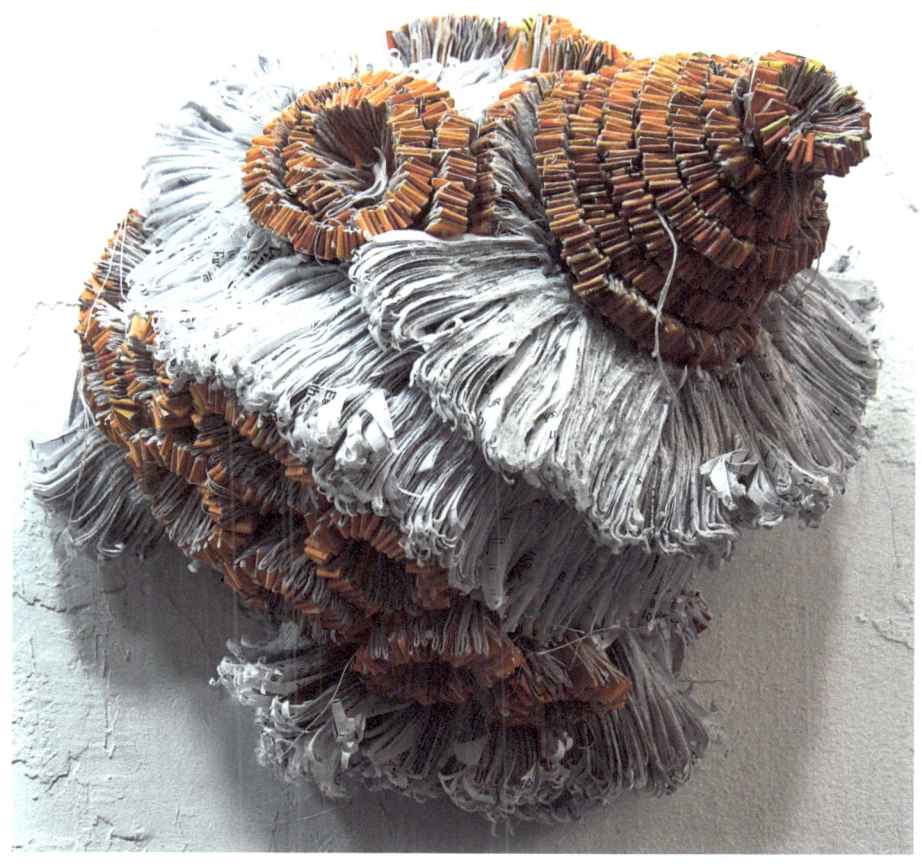

Jaynie Crimmins
Untitled 1: 2014: 9" x 9" x 5"D, shredded household mail, thread over armature

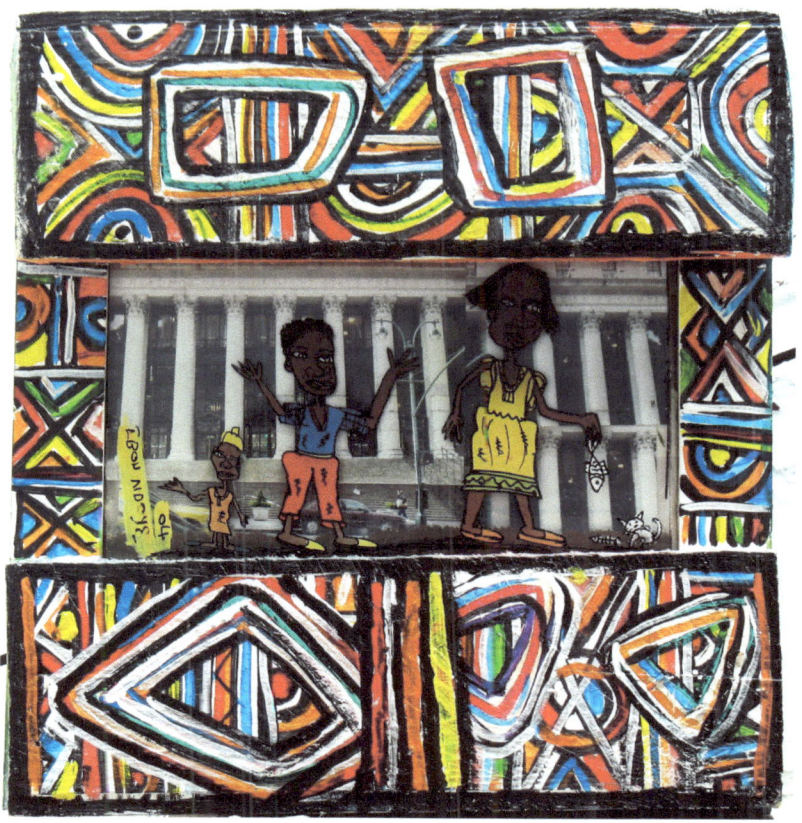

Ibou Ndoye, Feeding her cat in NYC, broken glass painting .wood, digital, Photography, 3 x12 2004

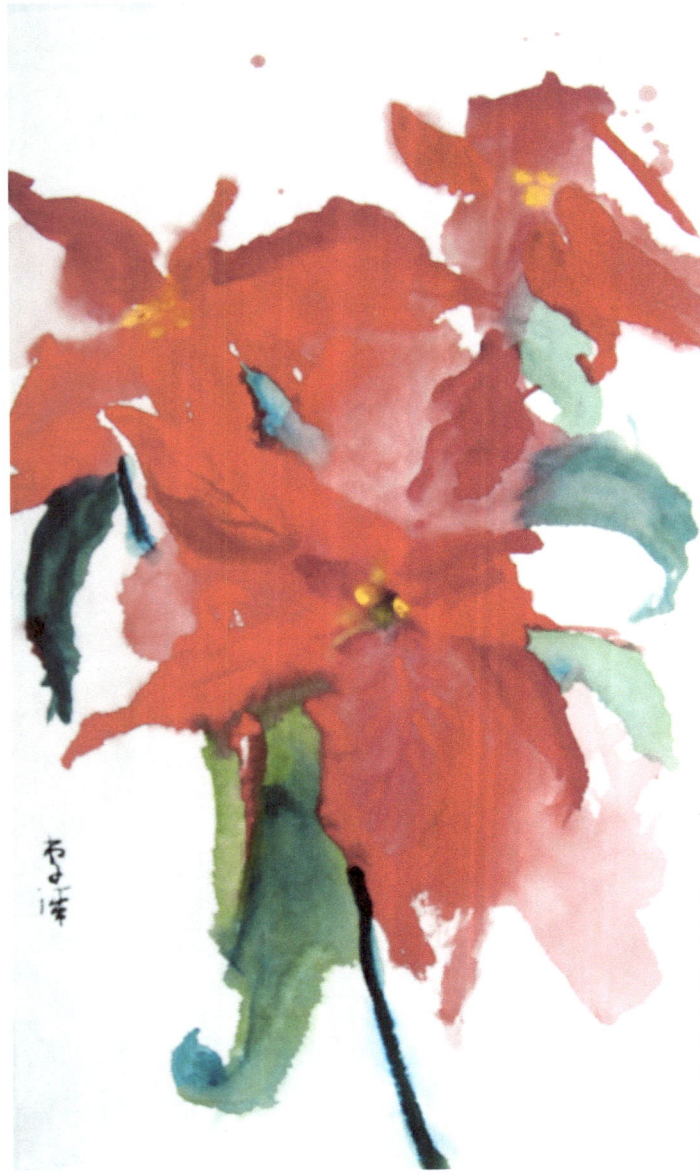

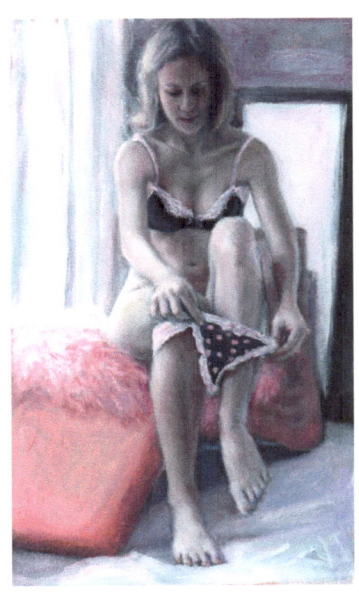

Michelle Doll, Polkadots, oil on paper

Dierdre Kennedy , Poinsettia, sumi-e ink on paper

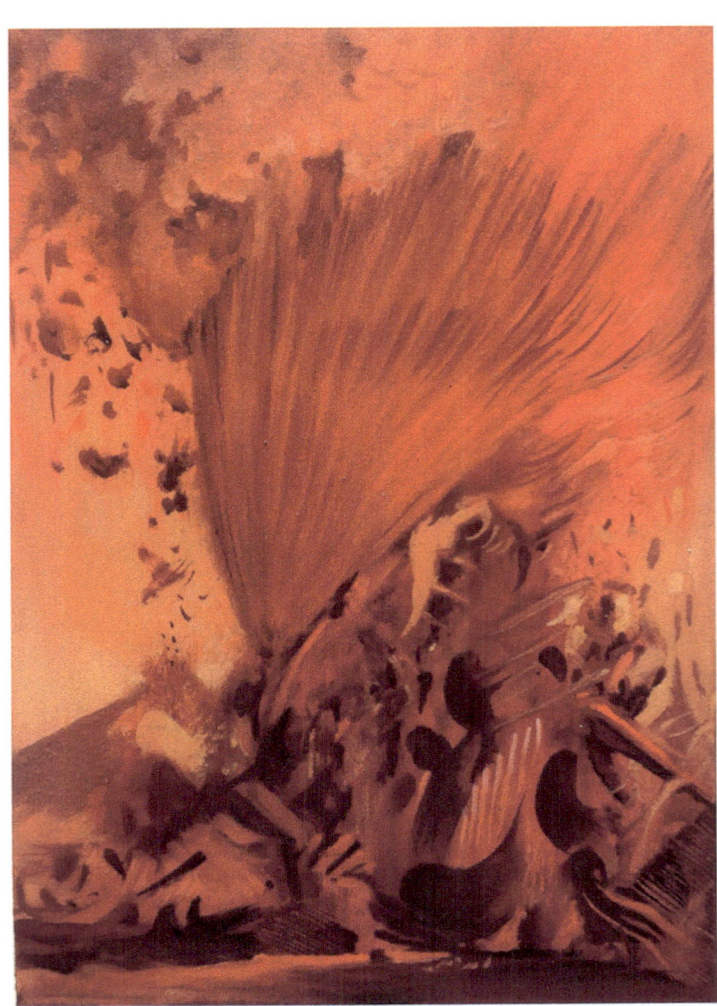

Fabricio Suarez, Volcan 2014 11 x 8 inches

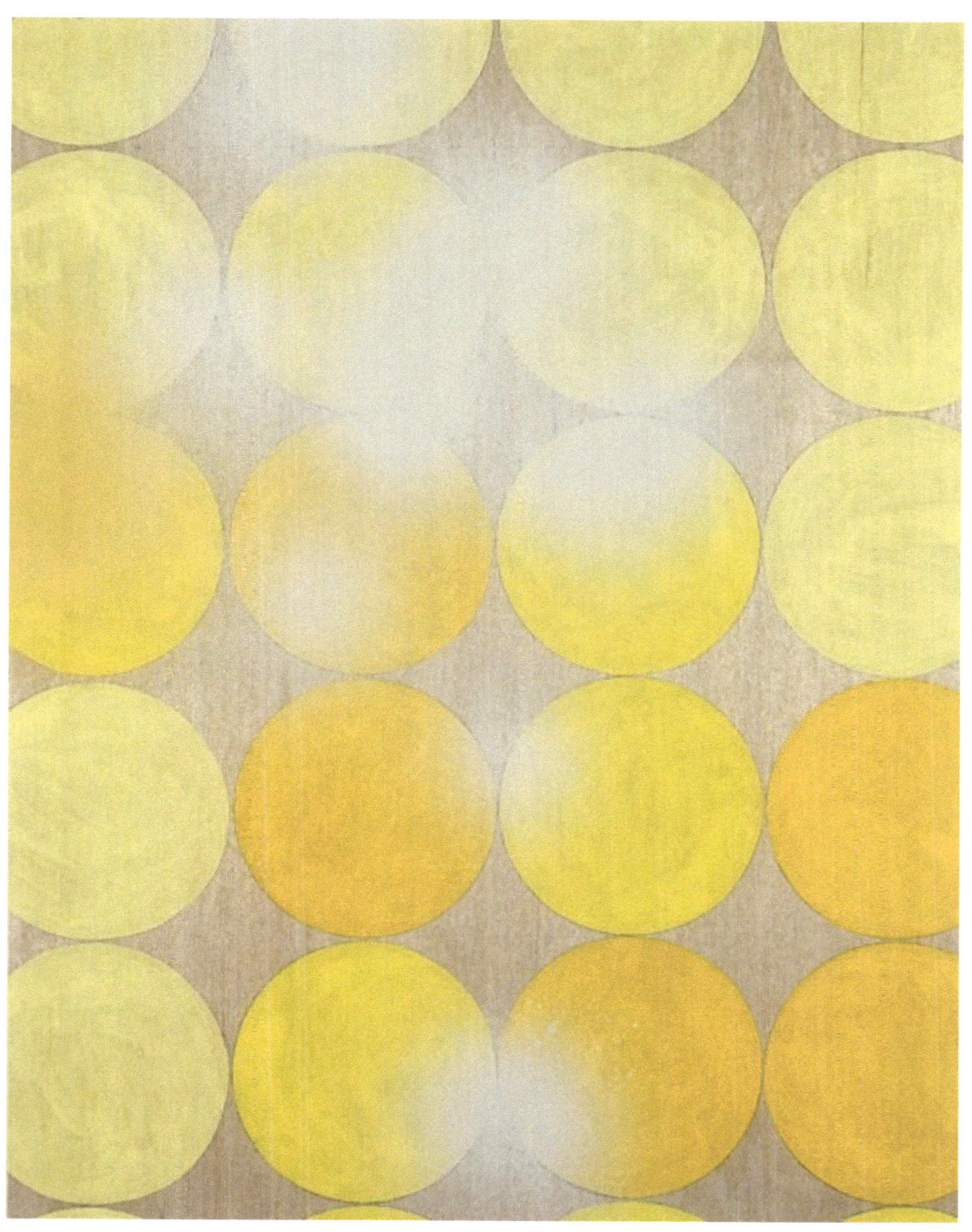

Michael Ensminger, Early Morning Panel 14 x 11 2013

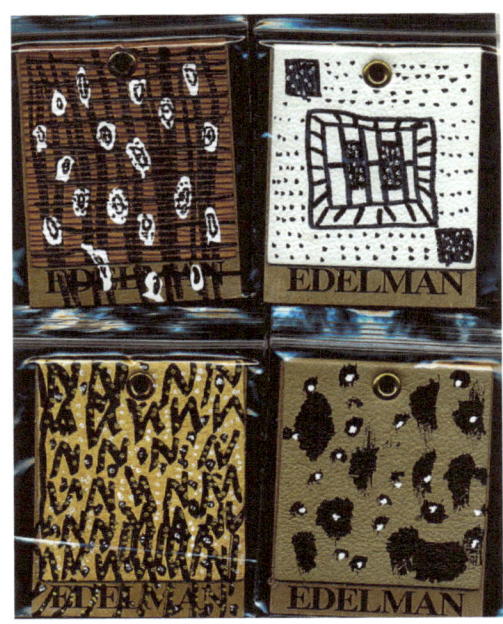

James Prez little drawings 2

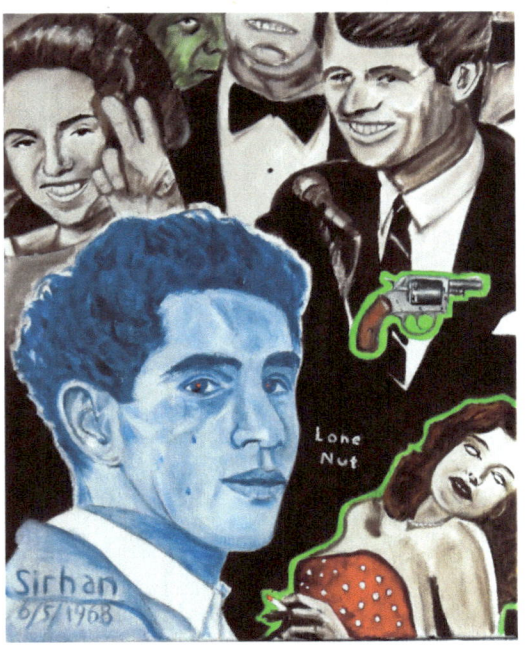

Robert Preston, Lone Nut -Sirhan,, oil on canvas

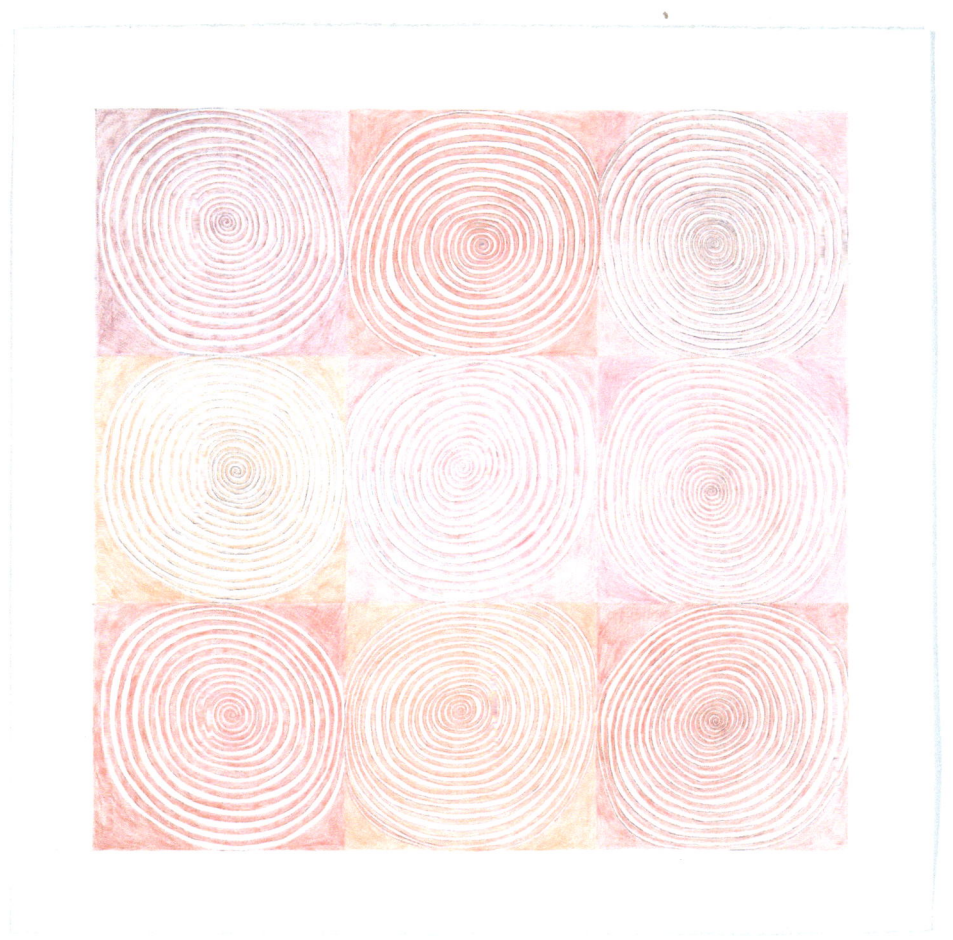

Eileen Hoffman, StitchWeave x 9a 30"h x 30"w 2007 Colored pencil on paper

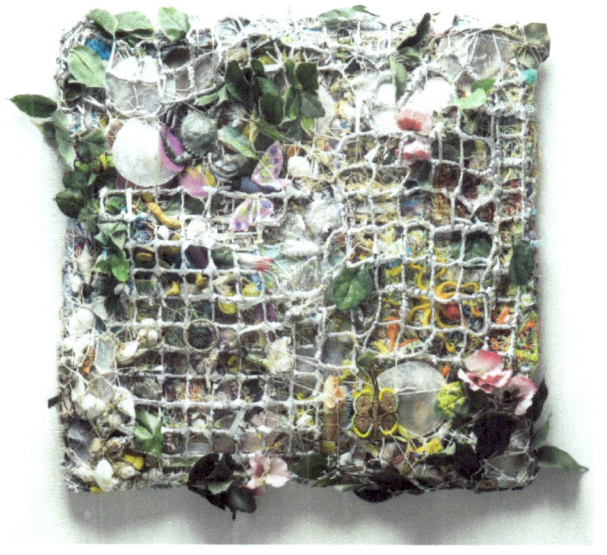

Maggie Ens, Atlantia, mized media

THANKS TO OUR DONORS FOR THE BIG SMALL SHOW

Victory Hall Press 180 Grand St Jersey City Nj 07302 december 2014
ISBN-13: 978-0692346501 ISBN-10: 0692346503

This program is made possible in part by funds from the New Jersey State Council
on the Arts/Department of State, a partner agency of the National Endowment
for the Arts, administered by the Hudson County Office of Cultural and Heritage
Affairs, Thomas A. DeGise, County Executive, and the Board of Chosen Freeholders.

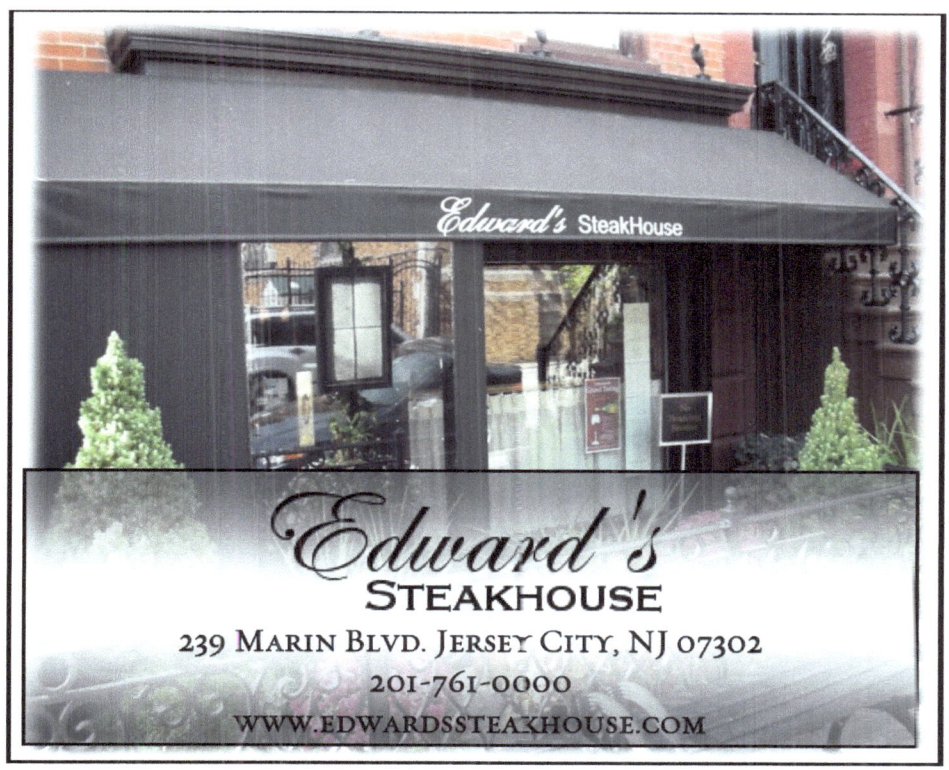

Edward's SteakHouse

Edward's
STEAKHOUSE

239 MARIN BLVD. JERSEY CITY, NJ 07302

201-761-0000

WWW.EDWARDSSTEAKHOUSE.COM

OFFICE HOURS BY APPOINTMENT

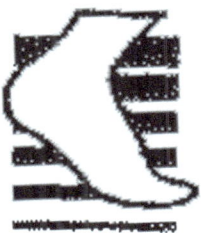

John B. Del Monte, DPM

PODIATRIC MEDICINE AND SURGERY

239 WASHINGTON ST JERSEY CITY 07302

TELEPHONE- (201) 451-4755
FAX- (201) 451-9459
DELMONTEPODIATRY@COMCAST.NET

Specializing in sports medicine and foot and ankle surgery with
over 20 years experience.
As Leonardo Da Vici said;
"The human foot is a masterpiece of engineering and a work of art."

Like us on Facebook@ Del Monte Podiatry

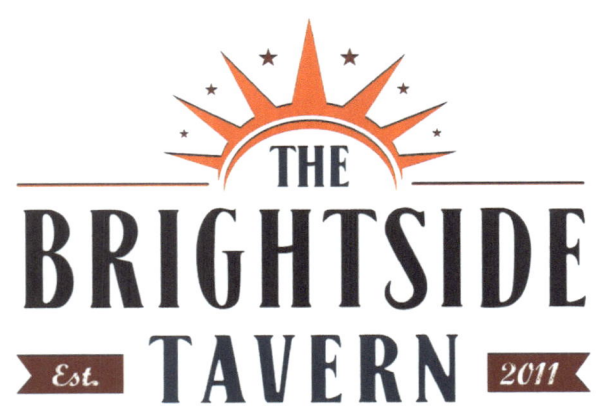

141 Bright St, Jersey City, NJ 07302 (201) 435-1234

CONGRATULATIONS

on the Second Annual
Big Small Show

Here's to a successful gala!
The Victory Hall Inc. Board

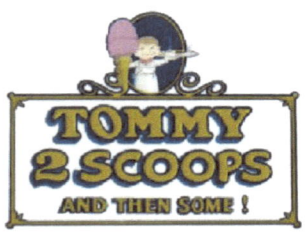

177 York St
Jersey City, NJ 07302
(201) 360-0791

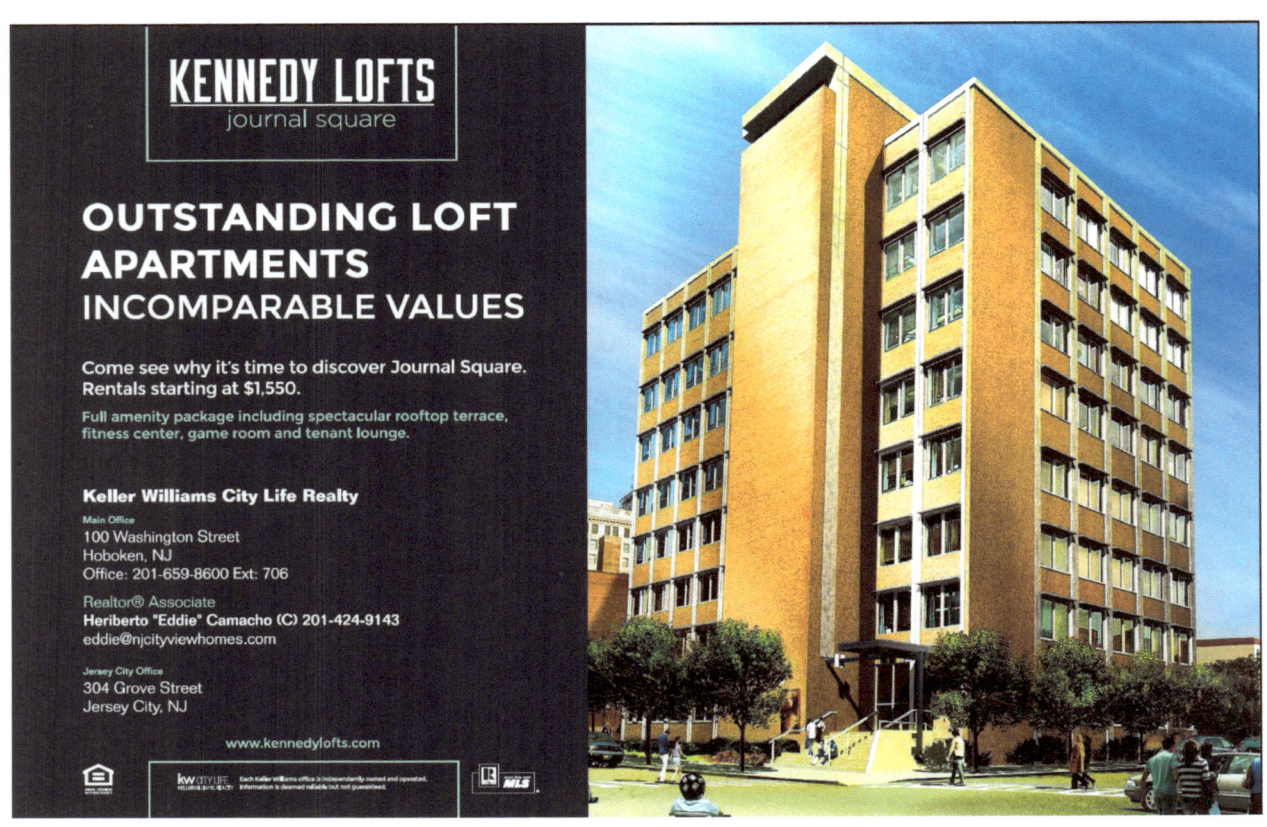